SCIENCE FAIR SUCCESS SECRETS

How to Win Prizes, Have Fun,

by **Bill Haduch**

illustrated by
Philip Scheuer

Science Fair
SUCCESS
SECRETS

and Think Like a Scientist

DUTTON CHILDREN'S BOOKS · NEW YORK

Library of Congress Cataloging-in-Publication Data
Haduch, Bill.
Science fair success secrets / by Bill Haduch; illustrated by Philip Scheuer.
p. cm.
Summary: Explains the scientific method and describes a variety of actual science-fair projects
in such fields as engineering, botany, behavioral science, and chemistry.
ISBN 0-525-46534-0
1. Science projects—Juvenile literature. [1. Science projects. 2. Science—Experiments.
3. Experiments.] I. Title: Success secrets. II. Scheuer, Philip, ill. III. Title.
Q182.3.H
507'.8—dc21   2002023536

Published in the United States by Dutton Children's Books,
a division of Penguin Putnam Books for Young Readers
345 Hudson Street, New York, New York 10014
www.penguinputnam.com
Designed by Richard Amari
Printed in China • First Edition
2 4 6 8 10 9 7 5 3 1

To Will and Casey, the kids who teach me plenty—B.H.

To my brother, John—P.S.

*"Sports has had its scholarship opportunities,
and now science finally has them."*
—ELAINE CHAMPEY, SCIENCE TEACHER, SMITHTOWN (NY) SCHOOLS,
WHO HELPED TWO STUDENTS REACH TOP NATIONAL SCIENCE FAIRS

Thanks to Diana Schulze of Old York School; Sr. Mary Ann Besitka, IHM, of Immaculata High School; Tamar Mays of Dutton Children's Books; Ann Korando and Michele Glidden of Science Service; Henry Ihling of the Branchburg Country Fair; the many students, teachers, and parents who answered my original cries in the science fair wilderness, including: Jeb Schenck, Sara Alvarez, Emily Keeler, Heather Jo Dixon, Freda Dixon, Ryan Montoya, Gordon Estabrooks, Nick Oberlin, Ginger Jacobs, Lori Painter, and George Ford; Amy Auchincloss of Discovery's Public Partnerships department; and all the participants in the Discovery Young Science Challenge and the International Science and Engineering Fair.

Special thanks and congratulations to the fifth, sixth, seventh, and eighth graders whose entries in the Discovery Young Scientist Challenge inspired the sample projects featured in this book: Matthew Edwin Calcagni, Maryland • Sharon Hsiao-Wei Chou, New York • Thomas Franklin Dial, Georgia • Donald Allen Dreschell, Georgia • Christina Marie Fazio, Maryland • David Grassi, Pennsylvania • Alyssa Marie Hapgood, Oklahoma • Vincent Yung Ling, Georgia • Bryan Richard Noel, California • James Morrow Olenyik, Indiana • Katie Marie Palmer, Missouri • Andrew Charles Peretin, Indiana • Amber Brianne Pollock, Wyoming • Mehran Michael Sadatmousavi, Arizona • Sean Jack Shanahan, California • Mazell Tetruashvily, Pennsylvania • Matthew Joseph Wiener, California • Randi Kathleen Wilson, Arkansas.

Also, thanks and congratulations to the high schoolers whose International Science and Engineering Fair projects are featured: Jessica Lynn Cordingly and Crystal Rose Hostetter, Wyoming; Michael Scott, New Jersey.

Contents

And Now a Message from Our Corporate Lawyer:

Neither the Publisher nor the Author or Illustrator should be liable for any damage that may be caused or sustained as a result of conducting any of the activities in this book without specifically following instructions, conducting the activities without proper supervision, or ignoring the cautions contained in the book.

SCIENCE FAIR SUCCESS SECRETS

A Memo to Science Fair Support Staff

After helping my son and daughter through seven elementary-school science fairs, I thought I knew something about the subject. Yessiree. I had glanced at teachers' science fair handouts. I had flipped through countless science fair books, picking out projects. I had stayed up late waiting for glue to dry. Sure, I've done seven science fairs. I've been a science writer for twenty-five years. If there are secrets to know, I know 'em....

Then I started the interviews and research for this book and stopped dead in my tracks. I was missing the point the whole time. Like many busy parents, I had never really taken the time to understand a fundamental secret: **A Science Fair Is a Practice Session for the Real World of Science.** It's really about helping your kid begin to think and work and approach life like a scientist.

When I finally understood what school science fairs were really about, it reminded me very much of the big medical and science symposiums I have visited as a writer—where real scientists display and communicate their big ideas. And I realized how understanding and participating in a science fair is probably one of the best foundations

a kid can have for future success in the real world of science. Not to mention how a project developed in the spirit of real science can go on to regional and national competitions and win major prizes and scholarships—sometimes enough to pay for four years of college.

Whether or not your own science fair emphasizes such things as the scientific method doesn't really matter. And whether your kids come away with fabulous prizes doesn't really matter. A science fair is really about uncovering and developing scientific instincts and talent. It's up to you and your kids to get the most out of the science fair experience. It might be your kids' first step toward a Nobel Prize—or at least a well-paying, fulfilling career that lets them buy you a nice house for your retirement.

—Bill Haduch

HOW THIS BOOK IS DIFFERENT

This book is about doing *science* for a science fair, not just doing *projects* for a science fair. The reason is simple. The biggest, most prestigious science fairs in the world—the ones that award enough scholarship money to enchant the trustees of MIT—emphasize the quality of the science behind the project, not the bells and whistles that are sometimes part of a project. Even the Discovery Young Scientist Challenge, a national competition for fifth through eighth graders, specifically looks at students' knowledge of science and their ability to communicate effectively about science. Though bells, whistles, and wacky gadgets often get all the "gee whiz" attention, gaining scientific knowledge and being able to communicate are the real secrets to science fair success.

Bill Haduch's Science Fair Attic Inventory *
Dinosaur display made of clay
Model tornado in two-liter bottles
Magnet display
Model volcano
Belt and pulley machine
Fingerprint-matching game
Tectonic plate display

*All of these projects were very nicely done, thanks. But at best, each gave my kids a few hours of experience with a specific scientific subject. None gave them any idea how a real scientist would approach studying volcanoes or dinosaurs or tornadoes or fingerprints. Those shortcomings are partly due to the fact that neither I nor my kids were able to read this book before I wrote it. Now we—and you—have no such excuse. ■

Kids! Don't Let This Happen in Your Town!

VOLCANO DISASTER CLOSES FILLMORE SCHOOL

by I.C. Plenty, Stuff Writer

Millard Fillmore School was evacuated and then closed yesterday after more than 300 model volcanoes erupted and caused an uproar during the school's annual science fair.

"It was an incredible scene—a complete disaster," said principal Frank Spanker. "Never did I expect all 317 students to bring in model volcanoes."

The eruptions, which began when the science fair opened at noon, sent streams of foul-smelling baking soda and vinegar flowing across tables and onto the gym floor, flooding hallways and classrooms. Students and teachers quickly ran from the building, slipping and sloshing through the hissing, bubbling, ankle-deep liquid.

"It's the end of Millard Fillmore as we know it," said Spanker, a handkerchief covering his nose and mouth. "We'll never get this smell out of here." Firefighters this morning were still pumping the last of the fizzing mixture out of the school basement.

The school will remain closed until further notice for deodorizing. Investigators are questioning students about what they call a "highly suspicious coincidence."

"I knew I was making a volcano and I knew my friend Danielle was making a volcano, but I didn't know everybody in the whole school was making a volcano," said fifth-grader Brianna Sanchez. "It's just too weird."

The Start of Something Big

Once upon a time your favorite rock star sang a song and someone said "Wow!" for the first time.

There was also a day when someone first noticed young Michael Jordan had the greatest basketball moves in school.

And this science fair you're getting ready for? It may be the first time someone sees the talent of some future famous scientist. Maybe that famous scientist will be you.

Don't go, "*Tuh*." The big, real world of science works much like a big, ongoing science fair. Various types of scientists from all over the world come up with wacky new ideas. They prove their ideas to themselves. Then they get together in cool places like Orlando, Florida, for a convention, and tell their scientific buddies all about it. And when they're done, they party— with platters of the biggest shrimp you'll ever see. ——————▶

The American Heart Association annual meeting, for example, is like a giant science fair for scientists who study the heart. They tell other heart scientists about their ideas in "poster talks"—that is, a scientist stands in front of a poster printed with details about his or her ideas and findings, and talks about what's on the poster. It's just like a science fair. The really BIG ideas sometimes get explained in auditoriums filled with thousands of scientists and news reporters from around the world. And as all these brains begin to understand these new ideas about hearts, they start to come up with their own new ideas. Soon progress is made in the science of treating heart disease. People live longer. Hearts are happy.

STUPID SCIENCE LAW
If it happens, it must be possible.

Albert Einstein enjoyed playing the violin. One day he was playing with a cellist (CHELL-ist—someone who plays the cello) and he kept missing his part. The cellist told Einstein, "Your problem, Albert, is that you simply don't know how to count."

$E=mc^2$

What Is This E=mc² Stuff Anyway?

Everybody talks about it, but few understand it. $E=mc^2$, a mathematical formula from Albert Einstein's theory of relativity, means "energy equals mass times the speed of light squared." Included in this theory are the ideas that the speed of light never changes, that time would slow down if you ever got close to the speed of light, and that matter and energy are not necessarily separate things. Einstein had an unusual ability to combine very deep thinking with very complex mathematical figuring. It's been said that only a dozen people in the world could really understand what he was talking about. Einstein denied this, but it's still a great excuse. If someone doesn't understand your science fair project, just say, "Guess you're not one of the dozen…"

The same thing happens in every other science. Botanists get together in Brazil to discuss their findings about rain forests. Geologists get together in Japan to discuss their findings about earthquakes.

The point is, when Albert Einstein came up with $E=mc^2$ in 1905, he didn't just get on his cell phone and tell a few friends about it. He *communicated $E=mc^2$* to fellow scientists and the world by presenting a paper to a scientific magazine. By learning how to develop and present a science fair project, you're following in the footsteps of the world's greatest thinkers. And that could be the start of something big. ■

It's Not Just About Winning
(But Is It Really About Shrimp?)

If you have a science fair in your school, consider yourself lucky. Not all schools have them. It means your school is giving you an opportunity to actually "do" science—not just talk about science and memorize stuff and cut open worms to look inside. It may be extra work for you, but it's also

In 1979 Sheldon Glashow won a Nobel Prize for his work with particles smaller than atoms, but years earlier he got his start with something a bit larger. He experimented with tomato plants for a science fair project.

If You Happen to Win...

Most schools hand out medals, ribbons, and certificates for science fair participants and winners. And if you win at your school, you may go on to compete in a regional fair, meaning the fair covers the best projects from several counties or even a whole state. At the regional and state levels, prizes often include savings bonds for hundreds of dollars and even college scholarships for the top winners. From there, you may go on to a national science fair. The biggest national ones are amazing—some give out millions of dollars' worth of scholarships and scientific field trips as prizes. Even elementary-school kids may find themselves winning "an afternoon with an astronaut" or a trip on a marine biology research vessel!

a lot of extra work for the teachers, so appreciate it. (Yeah, right!)

Different schools have different types of science fairs. In some you'll compete with other students for awards and prizes. These competitive fairs are often connected to larger regional and national science fairs. Winners at each level move on to the next level, much like sports play-off games. As the levels get higher, the prizes get bigger. Who needs TV game shows, anyway?

Other schools take a noncompetitive approach—no winners are declared, and everyone's work is seen for its individual value. Noncompetitive events are generally not connected with higher-level fairs.

As you'll see in the projects section, student works that make it to the large national fairs can appear as simple as measuring and reporting on the growth of grass under various conditions. Or they can seem as difficult as building a device to measure conductance quantization in metallic nanowires. (Don't even ask.)

Whatever type of fair you're in, and whether your project seems simple or incredibly complex,

THE ULTIMATE PRIZE

When you get too old to win prizes at science fairs, why not go for a Nobel Prize? They're considered the most prestigious awards for intellectual achievement in the world. There are six categories: chemistry, physics, physiology or medicine, literature, peace, and economics. Winners receive gold medals, diplomas, and recently more than $1 million. Entry forms are probably not available at your school.

11

it's your job to get the most out of the experience. Even if you don't win—or if they don't choose winners—you're learning to think like a scientist, act like a scientist, organize things like a scientist, talk like a scientist, tie your sneakers like a scientist. If you ever actually become a scientist, you'll be that far ahead of the game. And wait until you go to your first real scientists' convention and they bring out those huge platters of shrimp… ■

Go for the Gold

The "Olympics" of science fairs is the International Science and Engineering Fair (ISEF), held in a different city each year. It's for high school students who move up from five hundred regional science fairs in all fifty states and forty countries. Fairs at this level offer top scholarship prizes in the $100,000 range, with combined loot reaching $4 million.

For fifth through eighth graders, there's the Discovery Young Scientist Challenge (DYSC). Sponsored by the Discovery Channel, it gives younger kids a shot at big-time science fair competition. By 2001, top scholarship awards for DYSC winners had reached the $10,000 level. Not bad for kids who haven't yet reached high school! Twenty inspiring real-world projects from DYSC and ISEF are featured in the project section of this book.

Not Just Terrific... Scientific!

Some people expect to see spectacular stuff at a science fair—homemade hovercrafts that can float passengers through school hallways; X-ray vision devices that actually let you see through people's clothes; real working human transporter rooms as seen on *Star Trek*. But dazzling yourself and your friends is not really what a science fair is all about.

It's a lot simpler than that.

The best science fair projects really involve answering a question about something that makes you curious and proving to people that your answer is correct.

It's about doing science and communicating what you did.

That's how real scientists approach their jobs, and more than anything, a science fair is supposed to give you a taste of working like a real scientist.

For example, everyone loves blowing up a balloon, letting it go, and watching it dart crazily all over the room. Ha-ha! Let me do it! Gimme it! It's mine! Mom! ⟶

> The youngest person to be granted a patent is a four-year-old girl from Houston, Texas, who figured out how to use toy suction cups to pull open cabinet doors. With the help of her parents (a lot of help, no doubt), she patented a device that looks sort of like a little toilet plunger. It's intended to help handicapped people open cabinets.

Got a Patent on That?

Having the facts and figures on making a balloon hover is valuable information. Who knows? A toy-making company might use your ideas to design a hovering skateboard. That's why some kids in science fairs actually get government patents on their ideas. That way someone can't just take your idea and make a billion dollars on it while you're sitting on a curb whistling a dopey tune. Having a patent means only you—or someone you choose—can make, sell, or use your invention for up to twenty years. Getting a patent isn't easy, though. You'll need a lawyer, and you can expect to pay the U.S. Patent and Trademark Office at least $4,000 over the twenty years. Better get a paper route!

But have you ever wondered how much stuff you could attach to the balloon before it got too heavy to take off? And how about if you attached just the right amount of stuff to the balloon, with the perfect balance. When you let the balloon go, would it just hover in the air? Hmmm...Curious? That curiosity, ladies and gentlemen, is the beginning of a real science fair project.

In researching such things as how big a balloon, how much air, and how much weight, you are "doing" science. Whether you research it by reading or doing your own experiments, or both, you'll eventually learn whether a balloon can be made to hover. Believe it or not, a real science fair is more about telling people what you learned than dazzling them with the hovering balloon gizmo you built during your research. ■

STUPID SCIENCE QUESTION
If the temperature today is zero, and the weatherman says it's going to be twice as cold tomorrow, what's the temperature going to be tomorrow?

14

But Everyone Else Is Making Styrofoam-Ball Solar Systems!

Hooray for them. Your job, no matter what your friends are doing, is to follow the *scientific method*. If that sounds scary, don't worry. It's only because *method* is a very adult word that kids hardly ever use. "Pardon me, Douglas, but could you please share your skateboarding method with me?" Also, *method* has a very unexciting sound. Like your shoes hitting the floor at night. Meh-THUD! Don't let your heart be troubled. *Method* just means "the way something is done." And *scientific method* just means "the way science is done."

THE WAY SCIENCE IS DONE:
THE SCIENTIFIC METHOD IN 12 EASY STEPS

1. See, hear, taste, smell, and feel stuff and realize something makes you curious.

2. Read, learn, and think as much as you can about the thing that makes you curious.

3. Understand that one of two things may happen:

A) You're not curious anymore. This is good. Your research taught you something. You're smarter and wiser and you may now return to your regularly scheduled TV programs.

15

B) You're still curious. This is even better. You may have opened the door to the next big scientific discovery. Or at least a really cool science fair project. You may go on to Step 4.

4. Put your remaining curiosity into a single question you would like to answer.

Why the Scientific Method Is Cool

Did you ever draw a picture you didn't think was very good and yet someone came by and said, "Ooh, what a wonderful picture"? You got a funny feeling like "Who's kidding who?" That's because in the art world there's wiggle room. One person might think a picture or a song is great; another might think it stinks. And guess what? They're both right because who's to say? The world of science, on the other hand, deals with facts and truths arranged and explained so that there's no wiggle room. Or at least as little as possible. Doing science with the scientific method lets you say things for sure, and show people why you're right. It's a great feeling and very valuable. It's how medicine is made, and bridges are built, and spacecraft are launched. A science fair is really about learning to use the scientific method. In science, you don't want any wiggle room. A little wiggle can make a bridge fall down.

5. Take a guess at the answer. From now on, your job is to find out for sure whether your guess is right or wrong.

6. Decide what you need to do to find out whether your guess is right or wrong. Do experiments? Talk with some real experts? Do a survey of people in your town? Go to some special library that none of your friends have ever heard of?

7. Do the experiments, talk to the experts, do the survey, go to mysterious libraries—whatever it takes to satisfy your curiosity.

8. Think about your question from Step 4 and your guess from Step 5. You may have guessed right, or you may have guessed wrong. But now you know. And now it's time to tell the world.

STUPID SCIENCE LAW
"If you don't know what you're
doing, at least do it neatly."

9. Write down all the important stuff about your project. Describe your question, your guess, how you went about answering the question, and finally, *ta-da!* the answer to the question.

10. Shorten what you wrote so that all the important parts fit on a poster (or sometimes in a magazine article).

11. Use your poster or article to help you tell the world what you learned.

12. Take bows, accept applause, realize you're cool, have some shrimp.

In the next sections, we'll look in detail at each of these steps and see how the scientific method fits into science fair success. ■

5

The Scientific Method: The Real Secret to Science Fair Success

As any real scientist can tell you, understanding and using the scientific method is key to almost everything a scientist does in his or her job. It's a way to keep track of things and make sure everything is covered. And it also provides the material to help you communicate and prove to the world what you did and what you learned.

The judges in the biggest, most prestigious science fairs in the world say they consider two main questions when judging projects:

1. Did the student follow the scientific method and show scientific aptitude and skill?

2. Did the student communicate the project effectively? Notice there's nothing in there about having flashing lights on your poster. Following the scientific method and being able to describe what you did—that's what it's all about.

STEP 1: <u>CURIOSITY. YOU'VE GOT TO EXPERIENCE IT.</u>

Maybe you've heard that curiosity killed the cat. Maybe you've read the Curious George books. But have you ever

Fields Medal and "genius grant" winner David Mumford got his start at science fairs. He won a big prize at age fourteen for designing, building, and explaining the science behind his own computer—thirty years before IBM officially introduced personal computers to the world.

18

wondered about curiosity itself? It's got to be about more than dead cats and little monkeys, right? What is curiosity? Where does it come from? Well, ask yourself this question: If you were sitting under an apple tree and got whacked on the head by a falling apple, what would you do?

A: Scream bloody murder.

B: Curse a blue streak.

C: Wonder why apples fall down and not up.

Most people would do A, B, or both. Sir Isaac Newton probably did *all* of the above. Then he went on to figure out the laws of gravity and wrote and told people about them. Three hundred years later we're still talking about him. Now, Newton had the same sense of touch that you do. It wasn't connected to some special "idea center" in his head that dumped out the laws of gravity when thumped by an apple. Newton simply felt something and then wondered about it. He was curious. It's a small first step, really, but many people never take it. They're too busy screaming and cursing.

Let's look at some of the ways curiosity—about the things you feel, hear, taste, see, and smell—can kick off a science fair project (or a billion-dollar idea).

SITUATION: You wake up *feeling* more hungry on some mornings than on others.

Q: Did you hear what the stupid guy took up at college?
A: He took up time and space.

One possible response: Keep an emergency bag of cheese twists on your nightstand.

The curious response: Wonder which kinds of foods keep your body satisfied through the night.

SITUATION: Sometimes the train whistle you *hear* across the valley is loud. Sometimes you can hardly hear it.

One possible response: Keep the TV volume up at all times in case the whistle is loud.

The curious response: Wonder if weather affects how sound travels.

SITUATION: Your little baby cousin *tastes* some foods and then throws them across the kitchen.

One possible response: Always wear a plastic smock while visiting.

The curious response: Wonder which tastes babies really like.

SITUATION: While using a microscope at school, you *see*

that bacteria are starting to grow again in a dish that was sprayed with a germ killer.

One possible response: Run! Run for your life! Bacteria are taking over the world!

The curious response: Wonder whether the few bacteria that survived the spray are now producing super baby bacteria that will survive the spray and have even more super baby bacteria (and eventually take over the world?).

SITUATION: You bend down, *smell* a brightly colored flower, and a bee nearly flies up your nose.

One possible response: You scream, your wig flies off your head, your eyes bug out, you go completely stiff and fall over backward. Just like in cartoons.

The curious response: Wonder what attracted the bee to the flower in the first place—the smell or the color?

Notice how the word *wonder* kicks off every single curious response? That's really what curiosity is all about. A sense of wonder. It's inside everyone. You just have to take the time to reach inside and feel it. Isn't that *wonder*ful?

STEP 2: PRELIMINARY RESEARCH. JUST LOOK IT UP.

Once you're officially curious, the next step is easy. If you know how to read, that is. Just look up the thing that makes you curious in books, in magazines, at the library, or on the Internet. Scientists call this "preliminary research." You might call it "browsing." It might be a book about diet, a Web site about sound, or one of your mother's old books about feeding a baby. You might ask a teacher for help, read about bees—whatever it takes to satisfy your curiosity. Remember to lean toward the scientific—if train whistles make you curious about the way sound works, don't look up *train whistles.* Look up *sound.* At this point, begin keeping a notebook of what you researched, where you looked, and what you found out. This notebook will be used throughout the project to help you remember what you did and, later, to help you prove what you did.

An Interesting Note About the Importance of Notes...

Did Alexander Graham Bell invent the telephone, or did he just remember to take notes? A man named Daniel Drawbaugh claimed that he invented the telephone years before Bell did. Drawbaugh's argument was so good that the Supreme Court was called in to decide. The judges gave the patent to Bell because Bell was able to show excellent notes and drawings of his work. Drawbaugh? He sort of forgot to write stuff down.

STUPID SCIENCE QUESTION
What if laughing gas really did laugh?

→ **STEP 3: ASK YOURSELF, "AM I STILL CURIOUS?"**

Oh, go ahead. Ask yourself. (Real scientists talk to themselves all the time.) If you're still curious about something after all your reading and thinking, excellent! That's where history-making discoveries start. Or at least a great science fair project. Go on to Step 4. If there's nothing more you'd like to know, well, then, uh…fine! You didn't waste your time. You can use your preliminary research to impress your friends and win TV game shows. But as for a science fair project, well, it's time to go back to Step 1 and find something else that inspires your curiosity. You need something you still have a question about.

STEP 4: ONE GOOD QUESTION, THAT'S ALL YOU NEED

Your curiosity may be vast. Your research may have made you even *more* curious about *more* things than you started with. But don't fret. In this step, we put a lid on the whole thing. That's because real science only tries to answer one question—or investigate one thing—at a time. (And you thought science was difficult!) This is where we →

Give Your Question the Egg-Timer Test

No egg timer? Then just call it the Three-Minute Test. Give your question three minutes of hard-boiled thought. Can you think of some way to get to an answer? Would it be an experiment that you can actually do? A survey of people that you can complete in time? More research? Don't expect to get to an answer in three minutes—just a way to get to an answer. *Dum-de-dum.* Okay, time's up. Do you feel good? Excited? Ready to do what needs to be done? Then you probably have a good question. Do you feel bored? Frustrated? Ready to watch TV? Then go back to your preliminary research and think of another question. Don't worry. You only blew three minutes!

define exactly which single question your science fair project is going to investigate.

A good science fair question often takes the form of: "What is the effect of (something) on (something)?" As in, "What is the effect of weather on sound?" Or, "Which (something) does (something) better?" As in, "Which paper-airplane design flies farther?" Or, "Is what we've heard about (something) really true?" As in, "Do kids really need more sleep than adults?"

How do you know you have a good science fair question? A good science fair question can actually be answered by *you*. It's not some pie-in-the-sky question that would require a 90-foot catapult or a suitcase of plutonium to answer. And it's not some goofball question about space aliens that no one can really answer.

On the other hand, notice the above question about sound and weather. You can begin to imagine

STUPID SCIENCE QUESTION
Do spiders know what we named the Internet?

ALIENS: red or green?

that you might get the answer by listening to sounds in different kinds of weather.

The "question" in a science project is often called the "problem." Relax. It's like in math when 7x8=? or 5% of 50=? are called "problems." No problem, right?

Answering the paper-airplane question seems almost too easy. (And too much fun!) But it can very well be answered by fooling around with different types of plane designs—experimenting, that is.

And the sleep question? You can probably begin by asking your friends and their parents how much sleep they get.

Good science fair questions lead somewhere. They don't just sit there.

YES   No

STEP 5: COME UP WITH A "HIPPO-WHAT?"

Hypothesis (high-PAH-theh-sis). It sounds scary, but it's not. And it has nothing to do with a hippopotamus. It just means "educated guess." Now that you have your question, you can use your preliminary research to take an educated guess at the answer. It can even be fun. Suppose in your preliminary research you came across a ⟶

STUPID SCIENCE QUESTION
Would the world be different if
Einstein had owned a hairbrush?

sentence in an encyclopedia that said sound can seem louder when it rains. You think about your own experience listening to a train whistle and agree.

You may now consider yourself qualified to take an educated guess about your question from Step 4: "What is the effect of weather on sound?" Your hypothesis becomes "Rainy weather makes sound travel better."

Hmmm. So you think rainy weather makes sound travel better, huh? If science had a voice, you would now hear two words come booming out of the sky:

"PROVE IT!"

"Well," you might say, "I read about it in an encyclopedia, and I remember something about a train whistle…"

SOUND SMART!

If you're going to be throwing around major-league words like hypothesis, you should probably know what to call more than one hypothesis—as in: I came up with two hypotheses (high-PAH-theh-SEAS). Now you know.

The U.S. Patent and Trademark Office says Thomas Edison's first real invention came in his early teens—an electrical cockroach-control system.

→ "SILENCE!" roars the Voice of Science. "That's just preliminary research! That led you to a hypothesis. A hypothesis has wiggle room. You must now test your hypothesis—prove it or disprove it—and get rid of the wiggle room!"

"Okay, okay," you say. "I'll test my hypothesis, prove it or disprove it, and get rid of the wiggle room."

NOTE: At this point it is not wise to mention to the Voice of Science that you think its voice would be even louder if it was raining. Just move along quietly to Step 6.

STEP 6: <u>DECIDE HOW YOU'RE GOING TO TEST YOUR HYPOTHESIS</u>

This is where you let your mind wander and think about all the ways you might test your hypothesis to prove or disprove it. You should already know from Step 3 that you're not going to need plutonium or a giant catapult. This is where you figure out what you *do* need.

There are basically three ways to test a hypothesis: experiments, surveys, and special research. ━━━━━━━━━━━━━━━→

Maybe You Need to Do an Experiment

We're not talking about a night in a musty basement with bubbling green liquids and sparking electrodes. An experiment for a science fair is just an activity you carry out until you're satisfied that your hypothesis is proved or disproved. It doesn't matter whether the experiment is simple or complicated. Experiments discussed at big national science fairs have been as simple as watching and measuring the growth of grass. And they've been as complicated as using real laboratory equipment to grow bacteria and study how well medicine kills it.

A Look at Planning an Experiment—the Needa List

Let's go back to the hypothesis in Step 5—"Rainy weather makes sound travel better." What would you need to design an experiment to prove this statement? The first thing you need is a "Needa" list.

1. You need rain. If you're not expecting any between now and your science fair, maybe you'd better rethink your project.

2. You need a way to hear the exact same sound from exactly the same distance in rainy weather and in dry weather so that you can compare the volume of the two sounds.

3. You need to make sure the only condition that's different while listening is the rain, or the lack of rain. If you listen on a rainy night and a dry afternoon, how can you know for sure it's the rain and not the time of day that's making the sound different? If you listen on a hot, dry day and a cold, rainy day, how do you know the different temperatures aren't throwing things off? Keeping everything the same except what you're studying is called doing the experiment under "controlled conditions," and it's a very important part of any good experiment.

4. You need a sound that you can control. Although it was a train whistle that originally gave you the idea, there's probably no way to control a train whistle. (Unless your uncle is a train engineer. In that case, let that lonesome whistle blow!)

5. You need to rely on more than just your ears when you listen to the sound. How can you really tell from day to day whether one sound is louder than another, especially if the difference is slight?

Wow. That's a big Needa list. But never fear. With a little creative thinking you may just come up with a plan for an experiment. And it might go something like this: ➝

Three Things to Remember About Planning Experiments

1. Don't be too hard on yourself. Just as your project should ask only one question, your experiment should try to prove only one thing.

2. You should plan on running the experiment more than once—in fact, as many times as possible. When you can show that your results turn out the same over and over again, it makes your project more believable.

3. Your experiment should be reproducible—no, it has nothing to do with babies. You should plan your experiment so that anybody can do it and get about the same results. The trick is to take notes and describe everything you plan to do in as much detail as possible.

On a dry day at 5 P.M. when it's 70 degrees outside, have your folks park their car about 300 feet from your open window. Put a tape recorder on the windowsill and have your folks blow the car horn while you record its sound.

Then:

On a *rainy* day at 5 P.M. when it's 70 degrees outside, have your folks park the same car in the same spot and do the same thing. If you record the sounds on the same tape, with the tape recorder controls set the same way, you should be able to hear if one sound is louder than the other.

Voila! (vwah-LAH—French for "There it is!"). A plan for an experiment! Using a car horn instead of a train whistle makes the whole thing do-able. Being sure to consider the time of day and the temperature and using a tape recorder gives the experiment "controlled conditions." And it might even be fun if your folks can see the humor in sitting in the rain and blowing a car horn. (Maybe you'd better warn the neighbors…)

Maybe You Need to Do a Survey

Sometimes you don't need to do an experiment to prove or disprove a hypothesis. You need to do a survey. A survey often takes the form of asking people questions or counting people, animals, actions, or things.

A project, for example, might involve people's earliest memories. Your preliminary research might have told you that most people's memories start at about three years of age, but you're still curious. What about really old people? When do their memories start? Your hypothesis is that they don't remember as far back because they have so much other stuff to remember. Well, there's only one way to find out, isn't there? Ask them. And that's a survey. To carry out a survey like this, you might visit a senior citizens' center and spend a few afternoons talking to old folks. They might even teach you a thing or two, you little whippersnapper.

You might get the idea for a counting survey when, for example, a loose shopping cart collides with your folks' car at the supermarket parking lot. Who's responsible for all these loose carts? Are men or women or young people or old people more likely to put a

STUPID SCIENCE QUESTION
How do you know when a lightbulb has an idea?

cart back in the rack when they're done? Or is there really any pattern at all? A few Saturday mornings at the parking lot, just watching and counting and taking notes, can begin to give you the information you need to test your hypothesis that the real problem is parents with little kids. They're too busy struggling with the kids to bother taking the carts back.

Maybe You Need to Do Special Research

So you have some weird idea that the pointy mountain behind your house is really an extinct volcano. Your preliminary research turns up no information about that particular mountain and nothing at all about volcanoes in your area. But the shape of the mountain and

some of the ruts along its slopes have you bugged. Couldn't those ruts be where lava flowed down millions of years ago? Your teacher has an idea. Why not call a geologist at the local university and ask him or her about this particular mountain. As it turns out, the geologist you talk to has actually been on your mountain, poking around, and she can tell you exactly why it never was a volcano. In fact, she has pictures and geologists' magazine articles that tell the story of the whole local mountain range—information that regular people usually can't get. You're able to disprove your hypothesis about the lava ruts—they were just caused by erosion. And as part of your science fair project, you give the people of your town their first real look at how that weird mountain got there. You're a hero! The mayor talks about naming the mountain after you. Okay, wake up. It's only a dream. The science fair isn't for two months.

STEP 7: SPRING INTO ACTION!

Believe it or not, the hardest part of doing your science fair project is over. Coming up with a good idea, a good question, a good hypothesis and then figuring out what you need to test your hypothesis is the hard part. If you've done a good job, you're well on your way to a science fair project that meets the highest standards.

At this point, just follow your plan. If you decided to do an experiment, carry it out. Then carry it out again—as many times as you can. Don't be surprised if you need some adjustments to your experiment plan as you go along. You may even do your experiment several times, realize there's a problem, and have to start it over again (the experiment—not the whole project).

HONEST ABE, INVENTOR

So far, Abraham Lincoln is the only U.S. president to own a patent. After being on boats that got stuck on sandbars and dams, he invented a way to use air pouches to float boats out of trouble.

Don't get discouraged. Real scientists sometimes need to run their experiments dozens, even hundreds of times before they're satisfied with the results. The whole point is you're working toward the goal of proving or disproving your hypothesis.

The same goes if you're doing a survey or special research. You may find after a while that you have to go back to ask extra questions or count extra people or do extra research. How much you do is not the point. The point is, does your work move you closer to proving that your hypothesis is either true or not true?

It's extremely important to take good notes as you test your hypothesis, whether you're experimenting, surveying, or researching. A real scientist does just about nothing on the job without writing it down. Dates, times, detailed descriptions of successes and screwups, good stuff and bad—you never know what's going to be important, so write it *all* down. If something *looks* interesting, you might want to consider taking pictures with a camera, too. And scientists' notebooks (think Leonardo da Vinci's) are always full of sketches.

STUPID SCIENCE LAW
If you smell an odorless gas, leave the room immediately.

STEP 8: <u>NOW THAT YOU KNOW THE ANSWER...</u>

Remember at the beginning of the project when you had to reach inside and pull out the curiosity? And then when you did your research you had to reach in again and decide whether you were *still* curious? Well, you have to reach inside one more time and decide whether your curiosity has finally been satisfied.

In other words, did your experimenting, surveying, or researching prove or disprove your hypothesis?

Either way, you learned something. You know more than you knew before. You reduced the wiggle room. And now it's time to tell the world.

STEP 9: <u>GET READY TO TELL THE WORLD</u>

If you've been taking good notes, you shouldn't have any trouble writing the "story" or report of your project. This is where you put *all* the details, starting from the beginning:

→

• How you came up with the idea and why it made you curious

• A full explanation of your question (or "problem")

• A full explanation of your hypothesis

• Everything you can describe about your experiments, surveys, or research. You should list all materials used, how you used them, and include any drawings, photographs, graphs, computer printouts—whatever helps explain how you tested your hypothesis. Pretend you're telling another person how to do your experiments, surveys, or research. In fact, another person should be able to take this section and use it as a handbook of instructions to do his or her own experiments, surveys, or special research.

• A full explanation of what the project showed you. This is usually called the conclusion.

• A list of any books, experts, or other sources you used to help you do your project. Listing *Science Fair Success Secrets* as the first book will automatically gain you extra points (extra points from the author and publisher; not necessarily from the science fair).

• When you've put all your information into the report, you should go back and sum up all the important parts on one sheet (no more than 250 words). This is called the abstract, and it will probably be the most-read section of your report. Here's where people will go to get a complete overview of your project in about one minute. Scientists often say they spend more time

Nobel Prize winner Walter Gilbert got his first chemistry set at age six, and turned his attention to mineralogy by eleven; when he was in high school he won a major national science fair by experimenting with metals used in nuclear energy.

perfecting their one-page abstract than they do on the whole rest of the report. Though it's usually written last, the abstract is almost always placed as the first section of your report.

• Give your project a title. Sometimes the title is the first thing you think of when planning a project; sometimes it's the last. The title's biggest requirements are that it captures interest and tells something about the project in just a few words. It can be absolutely straightforward: "Insulation: Which Type Is Best?" It can be be cute and clever: "Music or Noise? That Is the Question!" It can even be both: "Ants Go Marching Two by Two—Multivariate Analysis of the Physical and Chemical Communication of Formicidae Species." All three of the titles above were considered to be good enough to make it to large national science fairs.

Your teacher will probably tell you how to put the information together for your report, what headings to use, and how it should look. (Today almost everyone wants it typed on the computer, so go bug your paren…, er, that is, get your typing fingers in shape.)

STEP 10: CREATE YOUR DISPLAY

Your poster, or your display, or your presentation board (it's called all three) is your tool for telling the world about your project and what you learned. You stand by

Q: What happened when the chemist read a book about helium?
A: He couldn't put it down.

38

it during the science fair and use it to help convince the judges—and science fair visitors—that you know what you're talking about.

Your teacher will tell you how big your display can be. Widths are usually limited to three or four feet because space at a science fair is often tight. And height is often limited to prevent someone from bringing in a 12-foot-high display with a disco ball and laser lights on top that would make everyone else's displays look like chopped liver.

The most common arrangement is a three-panel backboard made of cardboard. The panels fold slightly to allow the poster to stand by itself on a tabletop. These backboards are available ready-made at many office supply stores. They really are the same types used by scientists and others who make their livings doing what you're just now learning to do. You can also make your own backboard out of plywood or foam board. Just remember whatever you make needs to be transported to and from the science fair without damage. If it's big, you'll probably have to design it so that it folds.

Yeah, how come?

Once you have your backboard, feel free to paint it some cool color. Just remember that much of it will soon be covered with information about your project, photographs, graphs, charts, etc.

These days the best way to prepare headlines and text for your poster is with a computer and printer. The most readable way to present areas of text is still black ink on white paper. Use a simple font like Times Roman or Univers at 14 points to 16 points—big enough to see, but still small enough to fit plenty of words on a page.

For headlines, you can choose a different font from the text, but use the same one for all headlines. A poster with many different headline fonts looks disorganized. Using a different color for your headlines is fine, as long as it's readable and you don't go too wild. You want people talking about your project—not your crazy taste in colors. Headline font sizes should be about 30 points to 32 points and readable from some distance. You can go as large as you like for the project title headline—you decide what looks best.

Your teacher will probably tell you what he or she expects to see on the poster, but it's a good guess you'll have headlines and text blocks covering your question/problem, your hypothesis, how you tested your hypothesis, your results, and your conclusion. You should be able to adapt all this information from your project report.

After you've written your headlines and text blocks, check them carefully for spelling errors. Then print the sheets. They should all be the same width, but you may have to trim them neatly for length with scissors or a paper cutter.

Now you should lay your display board down flat. Loosely arrange all your headlines, text blocks, photos, drawings, graphs, and other information on the board. Don't use any glue yet. Slide stuff around until things begin to look nicely balanced and not cluttered. See what fits and what doesn't, and don't be surprised if you have to change a headline to fit or print a new text block with shorter text. It's all part of the process.

When you're happy with the look, it's time to get sticky. One of the best ways to attach sheets to your poster is with artist's adhesive spray, available at office supply stores. It makes whatever you spray stick like tape, and you can even reposition the items later. It's best to practice with scrap paper first so you know how much to spray, and you should only work with it outdoors because breathing the spray is not a good idea. Rubber cement or two-sided tape may also work. Most regular glues and pastes will cause the sheets to wrinkle.

Along with your poster, you should plan to bring, if possible, any models or devices you used to test your hypothesis. This always makes things more interesting—people love to look at gizmos. You should also have a copy of your project report, separate copies of your

one-page abstract that you can actually give to the science fair judges, and your trusty old friend, your project notebook—even if it's all beat up. Some judges consider your project notebook to be the ultimate proof of all your hard work.

STEP 11: <u>IT'S SHOW TIME! (ALMOST)</u>

By now you should know your project inside out. You've done it, you've written about it, you've even made a poster out of it. But will you be able to explain it all to the judges?

Answer: Of course you will.

Science fair judges are often scientists themselves, from local colleges or corporations. They were in your shoes once, and now they're there to help you get started. You'll simply tell them about your project, they'll look at your materials, and probably ask you a few questions. It's often as easygoing as a friendly conversation, and when the judging is over, you may find yourself saying, "That was it?"

After understanding and following the scientific method and writing so much about your project, you're well prepared. But during the judging you also have the advantage of a giant "cheat sheet" right in front of you—your poster.

Nope, you shouldn't read directly from it like a script—that's too boring—but there's no reason you can't use your poster to help you find your place and know what to talk about next, as you explain your project. And pointing out pictures or drawings on the poster as you talk can help keep things interesting.

As you explain, the judges will try to decide how well you followed the scientific method and how well you communicate what your project is all about. To sharpen your communication, it's a good idea to run through your explanation several times before the big day. Having someone videotape you can help you see any trouble spots. You know, like when you say "you know" too much. Or like when you say "like" too much. Like, you know, when you say, "The experiment was, like, you know, really awesome."

Force yourself to speak slowly and clearly and without a lot of "filler noise." Often we think we hear gaps in our speech and try to fill them with strange noises.

like
UMMM
you know
AHHHH
like
MMMM...

Chester

U.S. Patent
188,292

EAR CAREER

Chester Greenwood had big ears that itched when he wrapped a wool scarf around his head in the winter. He didn't want to be cold. So in 1873, at age fifteen, he experimented with velvet, beaver fur, and wire; invented earmuffs that really worked; and became very wealthy. US Patent #188,292.

"*Ummmmm… ahhhhh…*" Actually, the people listening to us would probably never notice the gaps if we didn't make the noises.

And here's a little secret about questions: No matter how much you prepare, chances are the judges will ask you a question you can't answer. Don't just stand there with a dumb look on your face. Don't say, "*Duh.*" And don't say, "I don't know." Just practice saying this line:

"Sorry, I didn't come across that answer in my research."

"Sorry, I didn't come across that answer in my research."

"Sorry, I didn't come across that answer in my research."

It's a magic phrase that makes you seem scientifically smart even when you feel as dumb as a doorknob. And the scientists will love it. They'll wink at each other and say, "Yep, this kid's one of us!"

STEP 12: <u>ENJOY!</u>

If you followed the first 11 steps, you should feel ready when the big day arrives. A little goosey, maybe, but ready. You've learned something through your project that you're sure about, and you're ready to tell the world. What you learned this time may not shake the world, but someday, following these same types of procedures, you may come up with something that does.

In the meantime, have fun! Your own time with the judges is only a small part of your science fair experience. Here's your chance to see what other people's brains came up with, given the same instructions as you. There will be many surprises and a lot of laughs.

Kids who make it to the large national science fairs are quick to talk about the fun they have there. It's often the first thing they mention. Unless they're the ones who win the huge prizes. Then they talk about the prizes first.

The fun doesn't stop after the science fair. What you're really getting is just a taste of the world of science—how it works, what the expectations are, how scientists interact with each other. If you feel a sense of achievement and enjoyment, go with it. Someday you may find yourself in some exotic land, in the most amazing hotel, eating fabulous food and partying with a bunch of your best friends, who also happen to be professional scientists. You'll look around the convention floor and you'll say to yourself, "Gee. I haven't had this much fun since my grade-school science fair." ■

Real Projects That Rocked the World

Rocked some of the world's biggest, most prestigious science fairs, that is. The idea is simple. The following projects, most of them by fifth through eighth graders, impressed the judges at local school science fairs, went on to win awards at the regional and state level, and then got picked as finalists or semifinalists for the Discovery Young Scientist Challenge (DYSC). Also included are a few finalists from the Intel International Science and Engineering Fair (ISEF), so you can see that high school projects are not that different from the ones done in grade school.

If you're an absolute first-timer, you might want to try to copy one of these award-winning projects (one of the easier ones, that is). That'll give you a taste of how the real science fair process works. But these projects are not really meant to be copied exactly. They're meant to inspire and demonstrate how the process works. They're meant to show you where curiosity begins and how it leads to questions and hypotheses, which lead to research and experiments, which lead to conclusions and presenting conclusions. These projects are meant to show how kids your age actually "do" science.

Let the inspiration begin!

Spaghetti and Marshmallows

It's kind of like edible Tinkertoys—building stuff with uncooked spaghetti noodles and using miniature marshmallows as the connectors. By sticking the stiff noodles into the marshmallows you can make cubes, pyramids, even wacky cross-braced structures just about as big as you like. And when you're done, you can take your projects apart and have a spaghetti dinner with a marshmallow dessert. Wow, that's really using your noodle! But before you start eating, you might start thinking…How sturdy can these weak structures be? After all, they're just spaghetti and marshmallows! *How much weight can they hold? Can you actually build something you can (gulp) stand on?*

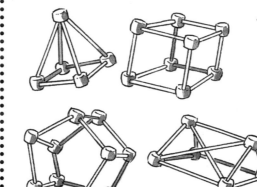

ACTUAL PROJECT TITLE
"Using Your Noodle"

QUESTION
Can weak materials be made strong through structural engineering?

HYPOTHESIS

Structures can be designed that support many times their own weight.

PROCEDURE

1) Build many different types of structures using triangles, squares, rectangles, pentagons, and helix shapes made from only uncooked spaghetti noodles of the same thickness and miniature marshmallows. Don't use any glue or tape.

2) Test each structure's strength by placing the same plastic bowl on top of each one and adding pennies until the weight makes the structure collapse.

3) Photograph and chart your results, noting how many pennies made each structure collapse. Knowing how each structure collapses will give you hints on how to make stronger structures by bracing, making parts longer or shorter, and so on. If the structures tend to sway and lean over under the weight, it's okay to place books or something heavy alongside the structures to brace them up. You're looking to make the structure collapse downward, not just slouch over.

4) When you find your strongest spaghetti structure, weigh the pennies it holds—and weigh yourself.* Figure out how many structures you might need to hold you. For example, if you build

* Be sure to include the weight of the board described in Step 5.

a structure that can hold 5 pounds and you weigh 100 pounds, how many structures might be required to hold you? Yes, it does sound like third-grade math class, and the answer is 20 structures.

5) Build the number of structures you think you need to hold you, place a board that can hold your weight on top of the structures, and climb (gingerly, very gingerly) aboard. Well? Are you standing on top of spaghetti?

Note: Structures fail if noodles are cooked!

CONCLUSION

The hypothesis is correct. With proper engineering, building materials can be made to hold hundreds of times their own weight. In the actual project, structures using only eight noodles arranged in a helix were able to hold seven pounds of pennies. So 11 spaghetti structures of this type were able to hold a 70-pound kid plus the board to stand on. Amazing!

WHAT IT MEANS IN THE REAL WORLD

Think of the spokes on a bicycle wheel or the skinny legs on a chair—lightweight materials are often used to hold more than their own weight. It's all in the engineering, but when you're on top of spaghetti, it seems almost like magic.

Better Cookies Through Science

DYSC Semifinalist

*Biochemistry,
Medicine,
Health, and
Microbiology*

WHERE THE IDEA CAME FROM
Wondering Why Mom Always Uses the Same Flour to Bake Cookies

Homemade chocolate-chip cookies. You know how good they are. But what if you wanted to make them even better? For your next batch you could change the recipe or the baking time or add more chips or add fewer chips. And guess what? There's a good chance you still wouldn't know whether you made a better cookie. That's because by the time you eat the second batch, you might be hungrier or in a different mood. You might say "yum!" while your brother says "yuck!"

If you're going to mess up the kitchen, you might as well know which batch is really better, don't you think? And that's where science pops out of the cookie jar.

ACTUAL PROJECT TITLE
"The Incredible Cookie Comparison Dilemma"

QUESTION
Does changing the brand of one ingredient (flour) produce real differences in chocolate-chip cookies?

HYPOTHESIS

Changing the brand of flour will affect the texture, appearance, and taste of chocolate-chip cookies.

PROCEDURE

1) Prepare three batches of homemade chocolate-chip cookies that are identical in every way except for one ingredient—the flour: use three different brands. Make about 30 cookies in each batch. Choose an expensive imported flour, a popular name-brand flour, and a cheap store-brand flour. Make sure everything else about the cookies is exactly the same—the cookie size, the baking time, the chips. Remember that when experimenting you're only supposed to change one thing at a time? You're only going to change the brand of flour.
2) After baking, place each batch in its own identical container. The containers should be marked A, B, and C. Only you should know the brand of flour that was used in each batch.
3) Ask 25 people to sample one cookie from each container as they answer four questions: Which cookie has the best flavor? Which has the best texture? Which has the best appearance? Which is the over-all favorite? Don't worry about getting volunteers. Offer people free cookies and they'll answer your questions all day. Keep track of all the answers.
4) After the sampling and the answering, you should have the infor-mation you need to rank the cookies according to flavor, texture, appearance, and overall wonderfulness. Remember, the only thing

different about these cookies is the brand of flour. If there's any evidence that people like one cookie better than another, the flour must be the reason.

CONCLUSION

The brand of flour does make a difference in the cookies' flavor, texture, appearance, and wonderfulness. In the original experiment, it turned out that the expensive imported flour created the overall-favorite cookies, but the cheap store-brand came in second. The most popular name-brand flour came in third. Surprisingly, the cheapest flour created the best-looking cookies.

WHAT IT MEANS IN THE REAL WORLD

Food company scientists use this type of scientific taste-testing to try and create foods that people will fall in love with. By changing only one ingredient at a time and testing the results, they can adjust their recipes to please the largest numbers of people. The right formula can be worth billions of dollars.

Help from a Dummy

WHERE THE IDEA CAME FROM
Loving Soccer and Wanting to Do a Project That Included It

Game 1:

Wow! Did you see that kick? I've never seen a soccer ball go so far! Wait a minute. Let me feel that ball....It's as hard as a rock! That's why it went so far....

Game 2:

Wow! Did you see that kick? I've never seen a soccer ball go so far! Wait a minute. Let me feel that ball....It's as soft as a doughnut! That's why it went so far....

What is going on here???

Time to get scientific....

ACTUAL PROJECT TITLE

"Does the Pressure of a Soccer Ball Affect the Distance It Travels?"

QUESTION

Same as the title.

HYPOTHESIS

The distance a soccer ball travels when kicked depends on the air pressure inside the ball.

PROCEDURE

Come up with a method to kick the same soccer ball exactly the same way, with exactly the same force, many times. All conditions should be exactly the same, except for changing the air pressure in the ball.

1) You might want to bug the manager of your local department store for the leg of a mannequin that they no longer need. Really. Sometimes they throw these things out or have some old ones in the back room, and that's what was used in the actual project. So what if they think you're weird? If you can't get a dummy's leg, think of something else that can "kick" a soccer ball the same way over and over again...A baseball bat? A landscaping timber?

2) In a place where you can control things like temperature and wind (hint: indoors), rig up a way for the leg to swing freely, the same way every time. In the actual project, Dad helped build a ply-wood frame with a steel rod axle for the dummy's leg to swing on. A landscaping timber could hang in a similar way. A baseball bat might be better swinging from a rope.

3) With a small air pump and an air pressure gauge, fill a soccer ball with air to its recommended pressure.

4) Place the soccer ball just at the toe of the hanging leg (or whatever you're using), in a good kicking position. You may have to rig something up so that the ball doesn't move. In the actual project, they used a small plastic bowl as a sort of kicking tee.

5) Pull the leg back on its axle until it's about parallel to the floor and mark its position on the frame. You want to be able to return the leg to this exact position later.

6) Let 'er swing. Measure and write down exactly how far the ball went from the point of contact.

7) Do the same thing 10 times at the same pressure and average out the distances for that pressure.

8) Adjust the air pressure in the ball by letting air out or pumping it in. In the actual project, they changed the air pressure two pounds at a time, going from a low of four pounds of pressure to a high of 12 pounds of pressure.

9) Repeat the kicking-measuring action 10 times at each pressure and average the distances out.

10) Compare the distances.

CONCLUSION

The hypothesis was wrong. Surprisingly, different air pressures had little effect on the distances the ball traveled. Also surprisingly, the ball tended to keep its shape at the different pressures. This is probably because the outside cover of a soccer ball is separate from the rubber air bladder inside. Keeping its shape probably helped the ball roll about the same distance each time.

WHAT IT MEANS IN THE REAL WORLD

There's no need to argue at soccer games about how much air is in the ball. About the score maybe, but not the air.

Cut the Grass Right, Will Ya?

WHERE THE IDEA CAME FROM

The know-it-all neighbor leans over your fence and shakes his head at your pop, who's cutting the grass. "If you cut your grass shorter, it'll grow faster," he says.

Will not," says your pop.

"Will too," says the neighbor.

"Will not," says your pop.

"Will too," says the neighbor.

"Guys, guys," you say, stepping into the uproar. "Stop your silly bickering. Allow me, an aspiring botanic wizard, to conduct a scientific experiment that will reveal once and for all who knows his beans about grass growing. Agreed?"

"Well, I guess," replies your pop.

"Gawrrsh. Okay," replies the nosy neighbor, sulkily going back to his house.

ACTUAL PROJECT TITLE

Determining Whether Grass Length Affects Its Growth

QUESTION

How does grass length affect its growth?

HYPOTHESIS

Grass probably grows fastest if it's not too long or too short.

PROCEDURE

1) Make three wooden frames, each a meter square. Frame 1 is four centimeters thick; frame 2 is six centimeters thick; and frame 3 is eight centimeters thick.

2) Place the frames near each other in the lawn, making sure each area of grass receives the same amount of sunlight and water. Anchor the frames with long nails, to be sure they don't move.

3) Every seven days for two months, cut the grass to the top of each frame with clippers.

4) Every week, measure a random ten clippings from each frame to see how much the grass has grown. Record your results and come up with an average for each frame.

5) After two months, compare the results for each frame.

CONCLUSION

The hypothesis was wrong. And so was the neighbor. The grass cut the longest grew the fastest.

WHAT IT MEANS IN THE REAL WORLD

Does your pop want more hammock time? Tell him to cut your grass short. The longer he leaves it, the faster it will grow. Landscapers can use this information to be more efficient. Additional testing might show that digging up the lawn and paving it over will reduce the need to cut grass almost completely. And it makes a great skate park, too.

Hamsterzzzzz

WHERE THE IDEA CAME FROM
Realizing Something About Hamsters' Sleeping Habits

Anyone who's ever had a pet hamster knows the deal—when humans are awake, hamsters are asleep; and when humans are trying to sleep, hamsters are gleefully running on their squeaky exercise wheels. That's because most humans are diurnal, or daytime creatures, and most hamsters are nocturnal. They naturally have their active hours during the night, and sleep during the day. But hamsters don't have watches. How do they know what time it is? Do they actually watch the light to know when to set their sleep patterns? And is it possible to change their sleep patterns by changing the time they see light? And how many sunflower seeds can they stuff into their cheeks, anyway? Oops. Sorry. Wrong hamster project.

ACTUAL PROJECT TITLE
"Can I Change My Hamster from Nocturnal to Diurnal?"

QUESTION

Same as the title.

HYPOTHESIS

I can make my hamster diurnal if I gradually change the light patterns in its environment.

PROCEDURE

1) Put your hamster and its cage in a room or a large closet where you can block out all natural light.

2) Put a full-spectrum fluorescent light in the room. These types of lights simulate actual sunlight. Plug the light into an electrical timer and set it—for now—to come on when the sun rises and to go off when the sun sets. This would make the lighting in the room seem just like a normal day.

3) Find a way to peek in on the hamster every 20 minutes for the first 24 hours. You want to make notes about when it's awake and when it's asleep during that first 24 hours when the lighting is timed just like natural sunrise and sunset. (So you can get some sleep, you might need some volunteers to help you do this through the night. Better yet—in the actual project, they put a digital camera in the room and programmed it to take a picture of the hamster every 20 minutes!)

4) Your job for the next 48 days is to take care of the hamster as normal, but set the timer back 15 minutes each day. That is, the light will come on 15 minutes earlier and go off 15 minutes earlier each day. (The idea is that every four days the hamster will experience "daylight" a whole hour earlier in its environment. After 48 days, daylight will be set back a full 12 hours. To the hamster, day and night have been reversed!)

5) Weight loss during the experiment (for the hamster; not you!) could mean the hamster is under stress. Every week, weigh the hamster to make sure it's doing okay. In the actual project, the hamster gained weight!

6) On day 48 of the experiment, when day and night in the hamster's environment have been completely reversed, call your friends (or get out your digital camera) again. It's time to monitor the hamster every 20 minutes for 24 hours and write down when it's up and when it's asleep. Why not make it a hamster sleepover and have some fun?

CONCLUSION

The hypothesis is correct. It is possible to change a hamster's sleeping times by changing the patterns of daylight. Changing the pattern 15 minutes per day does not appear to disrupt the hamster's well-being. The findings could be further supported by rerunning the experiment with multiple hamsters.

WHAT IT MEANS IN THE REAL WORLD

The ability to change sleeping patterns in living creatures might be useful in outer space or undersea activities where humans must take

turns staying awake. A day crew and a night crew could take turns running a space station or submarine, and both would feel as though they were functioning in daylight. It might also help Betty Lou, the cranky waitress down at the All-Nite Diner.

ABOUT ANIMAL EXPERIMENTS

Rules about using animals in science fair projects vary. Be sure to check with your teacher before beginning any project involving an animal. As a behavioral study involving a pet, this project was allowed by the International Rules for Precollege Science Research.

Launching a Career

WHERE THE IDEA CAME FROM
Wanting to Win a Rocket Competition

If you haven't heard about the school bottle-rocket craze, you will. It's all over the Internet, with whole Web sites dedicated to it. Bottle rockets are made of empty two-liter soda bottles, pumped full of air (and a little water) and blown skyward. It's relatively safe because the only thing flying around is a plastic bottle with maybe some balsa-wood fins. There's a lot of science involved, and a lot of fun. Many science classes have team competitions to see whose rocket goes the highest on the way up and "hang-time" contests to see whose parachute floats the longest on the way down. Parachutes can be tricky. A bigger chute might catch more air, but it's heavier, so the rocket might not go as high. But what if hang time had less to do with the size of the parachute and more to do with the material of the parachute? Maybe different types of materials provide different hang times, and picking the right one would give you a big advantage in competition. Sounds like a science project in itself, doesn't it? And it's sure worth a try.

ACTUAL PROJECT TITLE

"Which Parachute Material Will Give a Bottle Rocket the Longest Hang Time?"

QUESTION

Same as the title.

HYPOTHESIS

Among different materials used for bottle-rocket parachutes, nylon will produce the longest hang time.

PROCEDURE

1) Plan a bottle-rocket launching trial where all the variables can be controlled for nine separate launches. Use the same bottle rocket, the same air pressure and amount of water, the same launch pad, air pump, and pressure gauge, and make sure there's no wind.

2) Make three parachutes from three different materials—nylon, plastic, and cotton/polyester blend (like from an old dress shirt. And make sure it's an old one. Why get in trouble?).

The parachutes should be exactly the same size and shape. All strings should be arranged and attached exactly the same for all chutes.

3) Launch the rocket three times with the nylon chute attached. For each of the three launches, use readings from two stopwatches to accurately check the exact time that passes from liftoff until touchdown. Write down the stopwatch times and average them. Then figure out the overall average for all three flights.

4) Repeat Step 3 with the plastic and then the cloth parachutes.

CONCLUSION

The hypothesis was wrong. In the actual experiment, the cloth parachute provided the longest hang time with a total flight of 7.085 seconds. Nylon was second at 7.01 seconds, and plastic was not so fantastic—it provided a flight of only 5.46 seconds.

WHAT IT MEANS IN THE REAL WORLD

Using the information gained in the experiment had an immediate real-world benefit. The student used a cloth parachute on his bottle rocket and won a competition for his whole school district!

Does Left Get Left Behind?

DYSC Semifinalist

Behavioral

and

Social Sciences

WHERE THE IDEA CAME FROM
Watching Your Left-Handed Dad
Write So S - l - o - w - l - y

Did you ever notice the differences between right-handers and left-handers? Watch the way they write. As righties move across the page, their hands move ahead of the words. As lefties move across the page, their hands cover the words they've just written. Sometimes left-handers seem to write more slowly than right-handers, but is it just with writing? Or are left-handers slower at other things, too? It might be interesting to test righties and lefties for differences in reaction times. Let's see.... How about holding a food fight in the cafeteria? Would right-handers be quicker to bat flying pies out of the way? Hmmmm. Too messy. How about a showdown with an enraged king cobra? Would right-handers be quicker to leap out of the way of a deadly strike? Hmmmm. Too deadly. There must *be a way to* test reaction times that's neither messy nor deadly....

ACTUAL PROJECT TITLE

"Do Left-Handers and Right-Handers Have Different Reaction Times?"

QUESTION

Same as the title.

HYPOTHESIS

Testing 50 people will show that right-handers are faster than left-handers.

PROCEDURE

This test is built around a person's quickness to grab a dropped meterstick (it's like a yardstick, and there's nothing messy or deadly about it). You'll need 25 left-handers and 25 right-handers. The groups should be identically matched in age and gender. That is, for every 12-year-old male left-hander you test, you need to test a 12-year-old male right-hander. A test on a 35-year-old female left-hander needs to be matched by a test on a 35-year-old female right-hander, and so on. This lets you control the variables and eliminate the chance that differences in age and gender are throwing off your results. It's best to choose your left-hander first because a matching right-hander will then be easier to find. (Right-handers are almost 90 percent of the population.) Here's how the testing works:

1) Ask your victims to sit alongside a table and extend their "writing"

hand out over the edge. Have them open their hand so there's a five-centimeter space between their thumb and index finger. Tell them to be ready to grab the meterstick as you drop it between the space. You might want to have them practice grabbing it a few times.

2) When you're ready to test, hold the meterstick so that the 0-centimeter mark is at the top of the victim's fingers. Tell him or her to grab the stick as soon as it falls.

3) Drop the stick between their fingers. When they grab it, note the centimeter mark that shows just above their thumb. That's how far the stick fell before being caught. Write down the number.

4) Repeat Steps 2 and 3 four times for each person. Make sure you note the age and gender of the person so you can find a matching "opposite-hander."

5) Figure out the average of the four distances for each person. When you're done with all 50 tests, do an average for the whole group of lefties, and an average for the whole group of righties.

6) At this point, you'll know whether lefties or righties are faster—it's the group with the lower average centimeters.

CONCLUSION

The hypothesis was wrong. In the actual project, left-handers turned out to be 3 percent faster than right-handers. The project also revealed many other interesting findings: males were 15 percent faster than females, and people age 21 and over were 10.5 percent faster than people under 21.

TIME TO GET OUT THE CALCULATOR

The actual project went a bit further, converting the centimeter distance to time. If you know how many centimeters something fell, a formula called the gravitational constant can help you figure out the time it took to fall. The formula includes figuring out a square root, which math teachers (and calculators!) can help you with. The formula is $t = \sqrt{\frac{d}{490}}$ where d is the distance in centimeters, and t is the time in seconds. To get the time, all you need to do is divide d by 490. (Get the calculator!) The square root of that number will equal t—the time in seconds.

Righty

Lefty

ARE YOU LEFT-EYED OR RIGHT-EYED?

In the testing, the question of people being "right-eyed" and "left-eyed" also came up. Here's how to tell whether you favor your right eye or your left eye: With both eyes open, stretch an arm all the way out in front of you and point at an object across the room with your index finger. While looking at the object, close one eye. Did your finger seem to stay in place or did it seem to jump out of the way? Try the same thing with the other eye. The eye that sees your finger staying in place is called your dominant eye.

WHAT IT MEANS IN THE REAL WORLD

Because there are about nine righties for every lefty, the world is pretty much set up for righties. Even writing left to right favors righties because lefties tend to cover up the words as they write (unless you're a supersmart lefty like Leonardo da Vinci and you decide to write right to left). Most tools, like scissors, and even games are set up for righties (for example, in baseball, a lefty has to turn around at home plate before running to first base).

So righties tend to think lefties do things strangely. But this project shows that lefties may actually have faster reaction times than righties. So there!

The Sad Truth About Blinking

DYSC Semifinalist
Biochemistry, Medicine, Health, and Microbiology

WHERE THE IDEA CAME FROM
A Talk with an Eye Doctor During Career Day at School

Talk with your local eye doctor, and he or she will tell you that the average person blinks more than 10,000 times per day. Sweeping away dust particles is the big reason for all this eyelid slamming, of course. But are there other reasons? Sometimes people seem to wink and blink according to how they feel. Think of them batting their eyelashes at each other when they're falling in love or staring straight ahead when they're scared. Is blinking at all connected with people's emotions—whether they're happy or sad or scared or in love? Maybe it's time to make some popcorn and watch some movie clips and…er, do an experiment, that is, and find out.

bat
bat
flutter

ACTUAL PROJECT TITLE
"In the Blink of an Eye"

QUESTION
Do emotions affect how much a person blinks?

HYPOTHESIS

A person's blink rate will increase in response to a sad emotional stimulus.

PROCEDURE

In this project, you use a camcorder to videotape the eyes of six volunteers as they watch videos. The videos are four scenes that you pick from movies—one scene that's funny, one that's sad, one that's scary, and one that's romantic. You'll also need one scene that's just blank. A blank tape will do. Each scene should be two minutes long. Have each tape rewound to the scene you want to show. Don't tell the volunteers what the experiment is about. Make sure everything about the viewing environment is the same for each volunteer—the seating, the lighting, the background noise. You'll probably need a helper to switch the videos on the viewing TV as you run the video camera. The helper should remain as low-key and unnoticeable as possible. It's a good idea to practice the routine with your helper a few times before you start calling in the volunteers.

1) Seat the first volunteer and tell him or her to just sit back, relax, and watch. Have your helper run the blank tape for two minutes. Videotape the volunteer through the whole two minutes, focusing on his or her eyes.

2) Have the helper run the two-minute scenes from each of the four movie tapes—happy, sad, scary, romantic. Videotape the volunteer's eyes during the scenes, just as you did with the blank tape.

3) Repeat Steps 1 and 2 for each of the remaining volunteers.

4) When you're finished, the camcorder's tape should give you a good record of how many times each volunteer blinked during each of the scenes, including the blank scene. Count the number of times each volunteer blinked during the blank scene (this is your baseline blink rate). Then count the blinks during the happy, sad, scary, and romantic scenes.

5) Graph and compare the results.

CONCLUSION

The hypothesis is correct. For each viewer, the sad scenes produced the most blinks. (For some it also produced tears.) For half the subjects, the blink rate decreased during the scary scenes. The funny and romantic scenes didn't lead to any conclusions about blinking.

WHAT IT MEANS IN THE REAL WORLD

Moviemakers are always looking for ways to test whether their movies really grab people. Watching blink rates during the sad scenes might be an easy way to do it. Police might also be able to watch blink rates to check if a kid is really sad about cutting through his neighbor's yard—or just pretending to be sad.

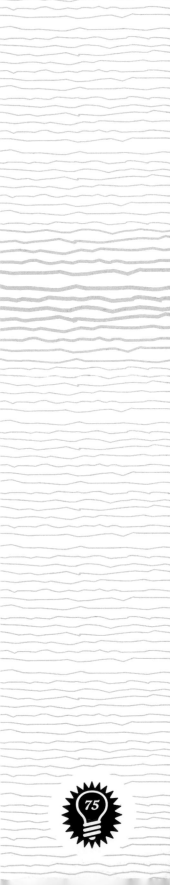

The Wurst Project

If you ever go to Germany, you'll notice that the food is the wurst—bratwurst, weisswurst, liverwurst, teewurst, blutwurst, knackwurst, bockwurst, gelbwurst, mettwurst, schmierwurst, pinklewurst. It's sausage—all kinds of meat, fat, flavorings, and mystery ingredients ground up together and spewed out of a machine. Most of it tastes great, especially the homemade kind. But sometimes you can't help but wonder what's in the sausage you buy in the store. That's where science meets the sausage, in this book's "wurst" project.

ACTUAL PROJECT TITLE

"Breakfast Sausage"

QUESTION

How do sausages vary in fat and water content?

HYPOTHESIS

Cheaper sausage will have more fat and water because fat and water are less expensive than meat.

PROCEDURE

1) Buy four brands of breakfast sausage, two one-pound packages of each. The prices should vary from the most expensive to the cheapest. All sausages should be about the same thickness.

2) Using a scale that measures in grams, weigh a plate that you'll later weigh sausage in, a bowl that you'll weigh sausage grease in, and paper towel sheets that you'll use to wipe up the remaining grease. (You may decide you'll use a wad of four or more paper towels at a time, but plan on using the same amount every time.) Write down the weights. You'll later subtract these weights from any sausage or grease you weigh.

3) Weigh each brand of sausage without the packaging, just before cooking it in a pan. Write down the weight.

4) Starting with a room-temperature pan, cook one package of the least expensive brand until it's considered cooked to eat. Don't make the heat so high that grease splashes all over the place. Note the stove setting and the time of cooking and write them down. Move the pan to a cool burner and let everything cool down so you don't burn yourself.

5) Take the cooked sausage out of the pan, wipe it with the paper

77

towels mentioned in Step 2, and weigh the sausage. Write down the weight. Also save the paper towels.

6) Pour the sausage grease into the bowl mentioned in Step 2. Weigh the grease and write down the weight.

7) Use the paper towels to wipe the grease from the pan, the grease from the plate, and the grease from the bowl. Weigh the greasy paper towels. *Eeeewww!* Write down the weight.

8) Dispose of the grease. (Not down the sink! Ask your folks. Sometimes it's best to dump it in a paper bag filled with balls of newspaper.) Wash everything you used. If you want to do an informal taste test later, put the cooked sausage in the refrigerator. If you can't help yourself, just chow down now!

9) Repeat Steps 3 through 8 for each brand of sausage. Make sure the cooking heats and times are exactly the same for each brand.

10) Calculate how much fat and water were in each brand. The formulas are:

- Fat in paper towel = Weight of greasy paper towel (minus) paper towel
- Total fat = Weight of fat in pan (plus) fat in paper towel
- Water content = Precooked weight (minus) total fat (plus) cooked weight.

Most of the water, by the way, is gone. It boils off during the cooking.

CONCLUSION

The hypothesis is correct. The cheaper sausages contained more fat and water; the most expensive sausages contained less fat and water. In the actual project, an interesting, but unscientific, observation was made—the cheapest sausage tasted the best!

WHAT IT MEANS IN THE REAL WORLD

People who don't want to get stuck throwing away a lot of fat after they cook their sausage may want to buy the more expensive brands. They'll pay more, but they'll get more—even if it doesn't taste as good.

BEFORE   AFTER

WHERE THE IDEA CAME FROM

Wanting to Build Faster Cars for the Pinewood Derby

If you've ever been a Cub Scout, or just hung around with them, you may have heard about the Pinewood Derby. The scouts carve small cars, about seven inches long, out of wood and race them down 30-foot ramps, competing with each other. Everyone has their own ideas about making the cars go faster. Some kids try to make the cars very sleek (aerodynamic) so they'll cut through the air. Some put graphite dust on the axles so the wheels spin faster. Some kids experiment with weights. Experiment with weights? *Hey, suddenly the Pinewood Derby sounds like more than a race—it sounds like a science fair project!*

ACTUAL PROJECT TITLE

"Weight Placement in a Pinewood Derby Car"

QUESTION

What's the best position for the accelerator weights on a Pinewood Derby car?

HYPOTHESIS

Weights in the front of the car will give it a quick start and make it go faster.

PROCEDURE

This is a quick and easy project, but it's best done with an actual Pinewood Derby car on an actual Pinewood Derby track. That's because you need a 30-foot inclined track and an Olympic-style timer that computes down to a thousandth of a second. If you're not a Cub Scout, just keep your ears open for news about the next Pinewood Derby in your area. Then get very chummy with a Cub Scout.

1) Build or borrow at least two Pinewood Derby cars of different designs. In the actual project, two cars with aerodynamic and non-aerodynamic shapes were tested.

2) Pinewood Derby cars are allowed to have weights placed in them as long as the whole car does not weigh more than five ounces. The weights and instructions for attaching them are available from the same place that provides the car kits. Place the weights in the front areas of your cars as described in your hypothesis.

3) Make arrangements to experiment on a Pinewood Derby track before or after the actual races. You'll need only about a half hour.

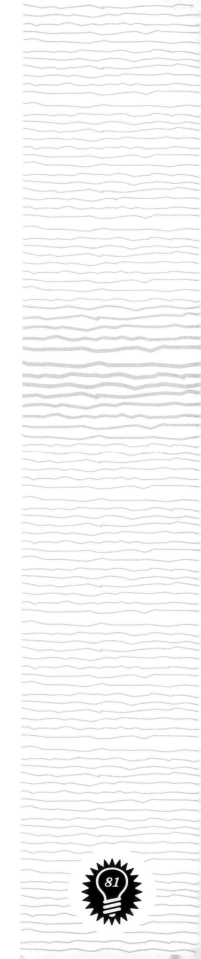

"Before" is better so you or your friends can use in the races what you learn in your experiments.

4) Run and time your cars on the track. In the actual project, each car was tested five times. Write down all the times.

5) Calculate the average times for each car and then calculate an overall average for cars with the weights in the front.

6) Move your weights to the back areas of the same cars.

7) Repeat Step 4, then calculate the average times for each car and an overall average for all cars with the weights in the back.

8) Compare all the times and chart the results.

<u>CONCLUSION</u>

The hypothesis is wrong. The cars with the weights in the back were faster on average than the cars with the weights in the front.

<u>BUT WHY? (THE CURIOSITY GOES ON.)</u>

Further research after the testing suggested an interesting reason for the conclusion. Because the track slopes downward, weights in the back of the car always start out higher off the floor than weights in the front of the car. This gives weights in the back of the car greater potential energy—a farther distance to fall. We're talking only a tiny distance farther, but when you measure over and over again in thousandths of a second, a tiny advantage becomes clear. In a race, a tiny advantage can mean winning!

WHAT IT MEANS IN THE REAL WORLD

Whether it's marathon racing or NASCAR racing, scientists are always busy looking for little advantages that make big winners. It might be finding a new kind of rubber that gives running shoes just the right bounce. It might be developing a new kind of paint that reduces wind resistance on racing cars. Even if the new ideas come about by accident, they're tested by using the scientific method. The science of racing can really be fun!

Some Like It Soggy

WHERE THE IDEA CAME FROM
Just Eating Breakfast and Wondering

In commercials, cereal companies often say their stuff "stays crispy longer in milk!" But some kids have a secret— they like their cereal soggy. You can bet there are some of these kids in your neighborhood. Maybe in your family. Maybe even…you! So what should you tell the crunch munchers versus the mush mashers? Is there a way to tell which cereals will really stay crispy longer? Is it the size of the cereal bit? Its thickness? The amount of sugarcoating? Maybe it's the type of milk. Well, hope you're hungry. Sometimes science lets you play with your food.

CRISPY

SOGGY

REALLY SOGGY

ACTUAL PROJECT TITLE

"Determinants of Soggy Cereal"

QUESTION

Does the amount of sugar, the size of cereal bits, and the type of milk have anything to do with how fast cereal gets soggy?

HYPOTHESIS

The type of milk, the thickness of the cereal piece, and the amount of sugarcoating will create differences in the time cereal takes to get soggy.

BUILDING A TESTING STAND
(NOTE: SEE ILLUSTRATION ON PAGE 86)

Before you start soaking cereal, you need to build a simple testing stand. In the actual project, a testing stand was built using six ice-pop sticks, white glue, and foam-core board (available at office supply stores).

1) Foam-core board usually comes in large sheets. You'll need only two four-inch squares. The board is soft, but get an adult to help you cut it anyway.

2) White-glue four of the ice-pop sticks to the edges of a foam-core square, two each on opposite sides of the square, as shown in the illustration. You can use a little tape to hold things together while the glue dries.

3) Glue the other foam-core square to the other ends of the ice-

pop sticks. This one should be about an inch from the ends of the sticks. Tape can help keep things together. Try to keep the whole thing basically in the shape of a cube. Let the glue dry.

4) Glue the two remaining sticks across each pair of sticks that are already glued in place. This makes the stand more sturdy. Let everything dry.

5) Poke a hole through the center of both foam pieces with a pencil. Wiggle the pencil around to make the holes big enough so that the pencil can slide easily through both holes.

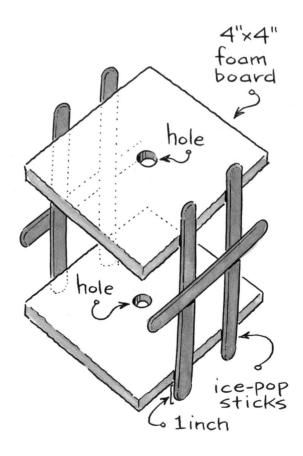

4"x4" foam board

hole

hole

ice-pop sticks

1 inch

PROCEDURE

The basic procedure was to soak different types of cereal in different types of milk, use tweezers to put the cereal bits one by one over the bottom hole of the testing stand, and use a stopwatch to time how long it takes a stick (like a pencil with a rounded tip) to push its way through each wet cereal bit. In the actual project, three sugar-coated cereals, three uncoated cereals, and three types of milk were tested—2 percent, skim, and goat's milk (honest!). They also used a dissecting probe (from a high school biology lab) instead of a pencil, but a pencil will work.

1) Pour a half-cup of milk into a measuring cup.

2) Choose 25 pieces of the first cereal. Pieces should be large enough so that they can be placed on the holes in the stand without just falling through.

3) Place the 25 pieces of cereal in the milk and start the stopwatch.

4) At two minutes, take one cereal piece out of the milk with the tweezers and place it over the bottom hole of the testing stand.

5) Place the pencil through the top hole and lower it gently onto the cereal piece. Either **A** or **B** will occur.

> **A.** The pencil goes through the cereal piece. Immediately try another piece. If the pencil goes through the second piece, that combination of cereal and milk has officially produced *sogginess*! Stop the stopwatch and record the time, the type of cereal, and the type of milk.

B. The pencil doesn't go through the cereal piece. Remove the cereal piece from the hole and wait 30 seconds. Place another cereal piece over the bottom hole. Try Step 5 again until A occurs and sogginess is achieved.

6) Repeat the procedure four times for the same combination of cereal and milk. This will help verify your results. Then move on to the next type of cereal in the same type of milk, using fresh milk each time. Then change the type of milk and repeat the test for all types of cereal. You can expect this to take quite a while, so don't plan to do it all in one day. In the actual project, some of the individual wait times for sogginess were over 10 minutes. Hey, nobody ever said real science was quick!

7) You'll end up with four "sogginess time" results for each combination of milk and cereal. Calculate the average time for each one. You should now know how long it takes each type of cereal to get soggy when soaked in different types of milk.

CONCLUSION

The hypothesis was partially correct. The thick, sugarcoated cereal always stayed crispy the longest, followed by a sugarcoated flake. But interestingly, another brand of sugarcoated flake was the fastest to get soggy every time. Uncoated cereals were about equal. And the type of milk didn't seem to have much effect. So in the end, if it's crunch you're after, the trick is *thick*.

WHAT IT MEANS IN THE REAL WORLD

Can you imagine a scientist in a white coat using million-dollar equipment to find out which cereal stays crunchy the longest? It happens. Procedures like this are going on in laboratories all over the world right now. Whether it's the "Fastest-Acting Cold Medicine" or the "Softest Toilet Tissue," every time an ad on TV says "tests show," this is the kind of test they're talking about.

This Project Is Soda Lightful!

> ### WHERE THE IDEA CAME FROM
> ### *The Yucky Way Your Teeth Feel After You Drink Cola Soda*
>
> **A**ctually this project is not so delightful at all. It's kind of gross. Did you ever drink a cola and then later feel your teeth with your tongue? Eeeewww! *It's like there's a sticky film or a roughness on them. And then you've probably heard stories about cola being able to remove paint and rust on cars. There are even rumors about putting it in engines to clean them out. Yikes! Cola's ingredients list shows things like phosphoric acid, citric acid, carbonic acid. These acids are in food, too. But when you drink a lot of cola, it's like giving your teeth an acid bath. Sounds damaging! What really happens to teeth when they're exposed to a lot of cola? Maybe it's time to brush up on the facts and get to the root of the problem. With a science project, of course.*

ACTUAL PROJECT TITLE

"Have a (bleep!) and a Smile!" (The real title mentioned a brand name, but we don't want to get the soda lawyers mad at us!)

QUESTION

What are cola drinks doing to my teeth?

HYPOTHESIS

A human tooth immersed in cola will lose some of its weight.

PROCEDURE

The first thing you need are human teeth no longer in a human mouth. Check in the phone book under "Tooth Fairy." He or she has *tons* of them. If there's no listing in your area, you can try "Oral Surgeons," usually listed in the Yellow Pages under "Dentists." Turn on the charm and tell them what you want to do. You'll probably come away with a bagful, but five to ten are plenty. Seven were used in the actual experiment. The other unusual thing you'll need is access to a scale that measures milligrams (thousandths of a gram). Pharmacists use them in drugstores. You'll only need to use the scale for a few seconds—first to weigh each tooth before the cola bath, and then to weigh each tooth after. You'll also need one can of the same brand of caffeinated, nondiet cola for each tooth you're going to test.

1) Weigh each tooth in milligrams and write down the weights. As an option, take a photo of each tooth.

2) Pour each can of cola completely into a glass and drop in a tooth. Make sure you know which tooth is in which glass.

3) After varying amounts of time, from one day to one week, take a tooth out of its glass and put it aside. Discard the soda (as if we had to tell you!). Write down how many hours the tooth was in the glass.

4) After about a week, the last tooth should be taken out of its glass. Now you can note the condition of each tooth and compare the condition to how long the tooth was in the soda.

5) Weigh each tooth in milligrams and note the weights.

6) Compare all information. If you took photos in the beginning, take photos now.

NOTE: In the actual project, the seven teeth came from the same person, and each tooth was taken out of the soda every day to weigh it and record the weights. These details are optional.

CONCLUSION

The hypothesis is correct. The cola had harmful effects on the teeth. All teeth lost a substantial amount of their weight during the test.

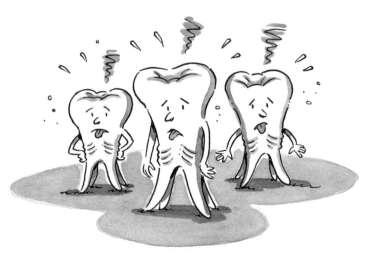

WHAT IT MEANS IN THE REAL WORLD

Scientists have gone to great lengths to create sodas that have no calories. It may be time to create sodas that are not so hard on teeth. Scientists would use tests similar to this to check their progress. In the meantime, remember this catchy cola tune: *Buh buh buh buh buh. Buh buh buh buh BRUSH!*

Slow Down That Woodpecker

DYSC Semifinalist

Botany and Zoology

WHERE THE IDEA CAME FROM
Watching a Woodpecker at Work

They're like flying jackhammers. They swoop in and peck into trees with their beaks, looking for bugs to eat. Sometimes their heads rat-a-tat-tat so fast you can't even see their heads—just a blur. The pecking sounds faster than a machine gun, way too fast to count, but really…how fast does a woodpecker peck? And do big woodpeckers peck faster than smaller ones? Asking a woodpecker these questions is useless. They'll just cock their heads, look at you like you're crazy, and fly away. The answers can be found through a more thoughtful, careful approach. Through a science project, of course.

ACTUAL PROJECT TITLE
"The Forest Is Never Silent"

QUESTION
Do larger woodpeckers peck faster than smaller woodpeckers?

HYPOTHESIS

Larger woodpeckers will peck faster than small woodpeckers.

PROCEDURE

It's impossible to directly count a woodpecker's pecks. They're just too fast for the human ear. This project uses a simple, indirect approach—get a recording of woodpeckers and slow it down. Nature stores and libraries have tapes and CDs of bird sounds, including woodpeckers. There are various ways to slow down a recording. Some tape players (like dictating machines and old reel-to-reel recorders) have a speed control. There are also many easy-to-use computer programs (including one built into many ordinary computers) that let you record sounds and change their speeds. In the actual project, sound was recorded from a CD and slowed down on a computer.

1) Get a recording that includes the sounds of various woodpeckers in action.

2) Note the names of the woodpeckers on the recording and look up their typical sizes in a bird book or on the Internet. Of the birds studied in the actual project, the hairy woodpecker (19.05 cm long) was the biggest, the Nuttall's woodpecker (17.15 cm long) was second, and the downy woodpecker (14.61 cm long) was the smallest.

3) From the original recording, copy exactly 10 seconds of each woodpecker's pecking sound onto a computer or variable-speed tape player.

4) Slow down the recording until you can count the individual pecks.
5) Write down and compare how many times each bird pecked during its original 10-second sound clip.

CONCLUSION

The hypothesis is correct. The large hairy woodpecker had the fastest pecking sound—210 times in 10 seconds—that's 21 times per second! The Nuttall's pecked 176 times in 10 seconds. The downy pecked 147 times in 10 seconds.

WHAT IT MEANS IN THE REAL WORLD

The project shows that with a little thinking, common technologies can provide answers to questions that were unanswerable not long ago. For example, 100 years ago, even the best-equipped scientist in the world would have difficulty counting a woodpecker's pecks. Now elementary school kids can do it. This "slowing down the sound" technique can be used to count many things. Ever wonder how many times per second your father's tonsils flap when he's snoring?

What to Wear When You Want to Be Warm

DYSC Semifinalist
Physical Science (Chemistry and Physics)

WHERE THE IDEA CAME FROM
Wondering How to Dress for a Trip to Texas

It started with a conversation about dressing for a hot summer trip. "Wear something that breathes" was the fatherly advice. And it set the wheels turning. Some clothes keep you cool by letting your body heat out. Some clothes keep you warm by holding your body heat in. Maybe a little science could help determine what kind of clothes keep you warmest. It's the exact opposite of what you need for Texas, but that's okay. Maybe next year your folks will take you to Alaska.

ACTUAL PROJECT TITLE

"Insulation: Do You Dress Right?"

QUESTION

Which of six fabrics is the best insulator of heat?

HYPOTHESIS

Among fabrics, wool is the best insulator.

PROCEDURE

1) Gather seven identical empty jars with screw-on lids. The jars should be big enough to hold about three cups of boiling water. Quart-sized canning jars would be a good choice.

2) Cut six identically sized samples of various fabrics. Each sample should be able to be wrapped around the jar exactly twice. In the actual experiment, samples of wool, felt, denim, polyester, cotton, and flannel were used.

3) Wrap each of six jars with one fabric sample. Secure the fabric to the jars with identical rubber bands on the top and bottom. Make sure there's still enough room on top to screw the lid down, but don't screw the lid on yet.

4) On a countertop, line up the six fabric-covered jars and the one jar with no fabric on it. The naked jar is your control jar.

5) In a small pan, bring exactly three cups of water to a boil. As soon as it boils, pour the water into the first jar.

6) Immediately take the temperature of the water in the jar. You can use an instant-read electronic cooking thermometer, available at houseware stores. To be even more accurate, you may want to ask your science teacher about the availability of a computer temperature probe. Write down the temperature and the exact time you took it. Use kitchen gloves to avoid burning yourself and screw the lid onto the jar.

7) Repeat Steps 5 and 6 for the remaining six jars, including the jar with no fabric on it.

8) Exactly 30 minutes after you took the temperature of the first jar, open the jar and take the water's temperature again. Write down the temperature and time, and close the jar. Do the same for each jar at its 30-minute mark.

9) Repeat the time/temperature routine three more times for each jar—at its 60-minute mark, its 90-minute mark, and its 120-minute mark.

10) Using the differences between the beginning temperatures and the temperatures at the 30-, 60-, 90-, and 120-minute marks (a total of five readings for each jar), compare the heat losses of the fabric-covered jars to the heat loss of the naked jar. Figure out the percent-

age of heat that was lost every 30 minutes. Compare and chart the results.

CONCLUSION

The hypothesis was wrong. Felt held the most heat the longest, followed closely by wool. Cotton held the least heat.

WHAT IT MEANS IN THE REAL WORLD

If you're trying to stay warm, felt and wool clothes can help. If you're trying to stay cool, try cotton. If you want to stay really cool, just remember the naked jar. But seriously, folks, testing fabrics for insulation properties is a big part of the clothing industry. This test can easily be expanded to include down feathers, fleece clothing, linens—you name it.

Wonder Worms

DYSC Semifinalist
Botany and Zoology

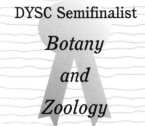

WHERE THE IDEA CAME FROM
Hearing Professional Athletes
Talk About Muscle Drugs

Training has always been the way athletes get faster and stronger. But every few years you hear about some miracle concoction that can produce giant muscles and amazing speed in athletes. People should absolutely never ever (never!) take any sort of miracle concoctions or drugs without a doctor's okay. Ten years from now you can wind up growing another head or something, and that would just be too weird. But what about trying the stuff on worms? Scientists often use very simple water worms for experiments.

Could miracle muscle drugs turn a slimy pile of squirming worms into a team of super-slugs?

ACTUAL PROJECT TITLE

"Which Worms Win? Do Creatine Monohydrate and Chromium Picolinate Affect the Locomotor Performance of *Lumbriculus variegatus*?"

Don't let that title scare you. Kids often use fancy words in their titles to make things sound more scientific, and it actually can make a good impression on the judges. Creatine monohydrate and chromium picolinate are just chemical names; *locomotor performance* means "the way something moves"; and *Lumbriculus variegatus* is the biological name of the worms.

QUESTION

Same as the title.

HYPOTHESIS

The two supplements will improve the worms' ability to move.

PROCEDURE

The first thing you need to do is get at least two hundred live aquatic worms called *Lumbriculus variegatus*. Now don't freak out—they're used in water-quality testing all the time. In the actual project, they were ordered from a company in North Carolina. You can easily order them through the Internet. You'll also need petri dishes and small containers (such as vials) to hold the worms. Your science teacher can probably help you obtain these items. Creatine monohydrate and chromium picolinate are available at health food stores.

1) When you receive the worms, you get to play with them. Pull a human hair out of a hairbrush and practice tickling the worms with it. This makes them move. With a little practice, you can get them

to move along the inside edge of a petri dish. Git along, little wormy!

2) Fill 20 small containers with a mixture of creatine monohydrate and spring water. Fill 20 small containers with a mixture of chromium picolinate and spring water. Fill 20 small containers with just plain spring water. Keep each group of 20 separate.

3) After playing with the worms and tickling them and getting them to move, place one worm in each container for an overnight stay.

4) For the next two days, take each worm out of its container and tickle it with the hair to get it to move around the inside of the petri dish. In a way you're "training" the worms to race.

5) After three days of training and three nights in their containers, you're ready for the real race. Tickle one worm at a time on your petri-dish "track" and measure how far each worm goes in three minutes. Write down all the distances and what containers each worm came from.

In the actual project, it was clear that the worms exposed to creatine monohydrate and chromium picolinate traveled farther in three minutes than worms kept in spring water. Earlier, during the preliminary research, the name of an Iowa zoology professor known for his work with *Lumbriculus variegatus* worms was found. The student e-mailed him the results of the experiment, and the professor wrote back with some suggestions to make the project even better:

A. Race each worm three times to get an average distance for each worm.

B. Increase the race times from three to six minutes to create greater differences in the distances the worms travel.

C. Do blind testing—that is, have someone else hand you the worms for testing without your knowing which batch they came from. That person should also take the notes. Blind testing eliminates the chance that you would spoil the results by "favoring" some worms over others. Hey, it happens!

CONCLUSION

The hypothesis was correct. Both creatine monohydrate and chromium picolinate appeared to increase the worms' speed. Uh, locomotor performance, that is.

WHAT IT MEANS IN THE REAL WORLD

There are many tests that scientists would want to do on a supplement that is supposed to make humans faster and stronger. Testing on worms would actually be one of the early tests. But would you ever imagine real scientists tickling worms with a hair to make them move? That's creativity, and that's what helps make this a successful science fair project.

Ice Is Not Always Nice

DYSC Semifinalist
Physical Science (Chemistry and Physics)

WHERE THE IDEA CAME FROM
Two Broken Teeth and a Busted Chin

Whoops! Boom! OWWWW!!!! *It's not the first thing you'll think about after a nasty fall on an icy driveway. But it might be the second thing.* How do we get rid of this ice!!!!!!!???? *The stores are full of ice-melting products. All the packages say they work great. But, really, you wonder: Which one should we use so I won't break any more teeth? Better hurry up and do a science project before the next ice storm!*

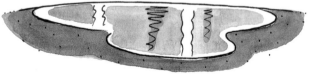

ACTUAL PROJECT TITLE

"Declaring War on Ice"

QUESTION

What is the most effective ice-melter, and what are the factors that make it work?

HYPOTHESES

1) Saturated salt solution (salt mixed with water) is more effective than salt crystals.

2) The higher the solution (the more salt mixed with water), the faster the ice melts.

PROCEDURE

The actual project tested popular ice-melters that use three different kinds of salts—sodium chloride (chemical symbol: $NaCl$), potassium chloride (KCl), and calcium chloride ($CaCl_2$).

1) Freeze 50 grams of water in each of 18 identical cups at exactly 0 degree Celsius and keep them frozen.

2) Weigh crystallized $NaCl$ ice-melter into three separate portions of 5 grams, 10 grams, and 15 grams. Do the same with KCl ice-melter and $CaCl_2$ ice-melter. You'll have a total of nine portions.

3) Put the nine portions in separate cups and add water to dissolve the salt crystals and prepare saturated solutions. (Politely) ask a chemistry teacher for help in creating saturated solutions.

4) Repeat Step 2, but this time don't add water. The salts in nine separate cups should remain crystallized.

5) Into each of the 18 frozen cups, place a quantity of saturated solution or crystallized salt. Make sure you write down which cup has which type and quantity. Return all cups to the freezer.

6) Every hour, check all cups and measure the amount of ice that has melted. In the actual project, the amount of melted water was measured each hour using a graduated cylinder. (For the saturated solution cups, be sure to subtract the original quantities of saturated solution.) Write down times and measurements.

7) Continue the process every hour until all cups have completely melted.

8) The fun part: Repeat the entire experiment three times. (Yep! Steps 1 through 7! Three times! And hurry! There's an ice storm coming!) Take averages of all results.

9) Compare the average melting times for each type, form, and quantity of ice-melter.

CONCLUSION

Hypothesis 1 is generally correct—saturated solutions of salts melt ice faster than crystallized salt.

Hypothesis 2 is generally correct, but there were some inconsistencies. The higher quantities of solution were generally faster.

WHAT IT MEANS IN THE REAL WORLD

It seems that the fastest way to melt ice at 0 degree Celsius is to use a NaCl saturated solution. But there's a problem. Although the testing conditions were well controlled, every driveway and weather condition is different. It would take a combination of experimental and real-world experience to really determine which ice-melter works best. In the meantime, consider staying inside and reading a good book if your driveway is icy.

A Concrete Idea

WHERE THE IDEA CAME FROM
Watching a New House Being Built

Houses are heavy things. Yet they often sit on concrete foundations, which are made largely of sand. Anyone who's ever been to the seashore or the desert or played in a sandbox knows there are all kinds of sand out there. It can be powdery or gritty. It can be tiny particles or large particles. Often it's a mixture of both. But what kind of sand makes the toughest concrete? A little preliminary research tells you that concrete sand is usually a mixture—particles of all sizes. But what if specific sizes of sand particles were used? Would the concrete be stronger or weaker, or wouldn't it matter? Time to get out the notebook and the wheelbarrow.

ACTUAL PROJECT TITLE
"The Effect of Sand-Grain Size on the Durability of Concrete"

QUESTION

What is concrete's durability when it is made with different sand-particle sizes?

HYPOTHESIS

A medium-grain size would give concrete the most durability because it has just the right amount of surface area for a high adhesive force.

PROCEDURE

The project tested the strengths of concrete "sticks" made with different sand-particle sizes. In the actual experiment, the wet concrete mixture was poured into lengths of clear plastic tubing to dry and harden, or "cure." After curing, the tubing was cut away, leaving the sticks of concrete for testing. Five sample concrete mixtures were tested, using equal measures of portland cement, water, and five different sand-particle sizes ranging from small grain to medium grain to large grain. (Sand particles are measured in "mesh" sizes. Masonry supply stores usually have various sizes available.)

1) Cut 15 plastic tubes, 0.95 centimeter inside diameter and 20 centimeters long. Seal one end of each tube with waterproof tape.

2) Mix a batch of concrete, using 150 milliliters of portland cement, 140 milliliters of water, and 300 milliliters of a sand size. Pour the wet concrete into three of the plastic tubes.

3) Repeat Step 2, using the remaining sand sizes. Be sure to write down which tube holds which mixture. You'll end up with 15 tubes holding concrete made with five different sand sizes.

4) Cure the concrete by placing all 15 tubes in the shade for five days.

5) After five days, cut open the plastic tubes. You should now have 15 concrete sticks—three each of five different sand-particle sizes. Mark each one so you know which sand-particle size it has.

6) Use two lengths of strong string to create a hanging device for the concrete sticks. One end of each string should be securely tied to a sturdy overhead support like a swing set or a tree branch. The other end should be a loop that will slip over one end of a concrete stick. When you're finished, you should have two parallel strings about 20 centimeters apart with loops on their ends. The loops should be about two feet off the ground.

7) Place your first concrete stick into the hanging device by slipping each end of the concrete stick into a loop. You'll end up with something that looks like a trapeze swing in a circus. Measure exactly how far apart on the concrete stick the two loops are placed. You'll need this measurement later.

8) With the first concrete stick hanging in the device and a meter-stick (it's like a yardstick) to measure distance, hold a roll of pennies above the center of the concrete stick and drop the roll. In the actual project, the pennies were first held 1.9 centimeters above the stick

111

and dropped. If the impact of the pennies doesn't break the concrete stick, raise the pennies a little higher and try again. Keep raising the height and trying until the concrete stick breaks. Make notes of all heights tried and the concrete stick's breaking point.

9) Test all 15 concrete sticks as in Step 8. Make sure the distance between the loops is always the same. Make sure you always begin by dropping the penny roll from the same height.

10) Take averages of the breaking point for each of the five sand-particle sizes. Compare and chart your findings. The concrete stick that withstands penny-roll drops from the greatest height has the greatest impact durability.

CONCLUSION

The hypothesis was wrong. The concrete with the largest sand size had the greatest impact durability.

WHAT IT MEANS IN THE REAL WORLD

If you ever want to make baseball bats out of concrete, use large sand particles. Heh, heh. Mixing and pouring concrete may just seem like a job for the muscles and not the brain, but there's actually a lot of science involved. Which concrete mix is best for tall structures, wide structures, wet structures, small structures? Years ago some-one had the idea to build a ship out of concrete in order to save steel. It sank, and you can still see the top of it sticking out of the water off Cape May, New Jersey. Think a little concrete science may have helped?

Wash 'n' Grow

DYSC Semifinalist

Environmental Science

WHERE THE IDEA CAME FROM
Trying to Grow a Garden During a Dry Spell

It's tough to grow a garden when it doesn't rain for months. When a dry spell becomes a drought, it can even be illegal to water the plants around your house. What about using recycled water, then? Water from washing machines just contains the dirt from your clothes and detergent. Can the rinse water that would normally be wasted be used to water the garden? And is there a way to get detergent chemicals like chlorine out of the water before you use it? Water you waiting for? Sounds like the seeds of a science project....

ACTUAL PROJECT TITLE
"The Effect of Recycled Laundry Water on Vegetable Plants"

QUESTION
How does laundry water affect plant growth?

HYPOTHESES

1) Seeds of plants watered with pure tap water will sprout quickest.

2) Existing plants watered with rinse water, especially rinse water containing chlorine bleach, will grow at a slower rate.

3) Letting rinse water sit for a week before using it will not change its quality.

PROCEDURES

This monthlong project is based on three procedures that use rinse water from a washing machine. In the actual project, one regular detergent was used, along with two detergents with bleach. Ask whoever washes your clothes to (please) alternate detergents and tell you what is being used so you can collect the rinse water. You'll want enough rinse water of each type available at all times to keep three soil containers moist enough to sprout seeds. You'll also need enough to keep eight existing plants happy. There are many different types of washing machines. Probably the easiest way to get the water you need is to turn off the machine right after the final rinse but before it drains. Wait until everything stops and use a plastic container to dip water out of the machine. Then turn the machine back on and let it drain normally.

PROCEDURE A

1) Prepare 12 identical soil containers. Plant 10 bean seeds in each of four containers. Plant 10 corn seeds in each of four containers. Plant 10 pea seeds in each of four containers. Make sure you label each container.

2) Keep the soil in one bean-seed container, one corn-seed container, and one pea-seed container moist with rinse water from Detergent A. The soil should be kept just moist enough to sprout the seeds. Keep all light and temperature conditions favorable for sprouting seeds.

3) Similarly, keep other sets of bean, corn, and pea containers moist with rinse water from Detergent B and Detergent C. The final bean, corn, and pea containers should be kept moist with plain tap water. This is the control set. Make sure you know what kind of seeds and water are in each container.

4) Every day for four weeks, check the 12 containers. As seeds germinate, write down how many and when. Chart the results.

PROCEDURE B

1) Set up a group of eight existing plants to test. In the actual project, four similarly sized strawberry plants and four similarly sized lettuce plants were used. The four strawberry plants were watered as needed with rinse water from Detergents A, B, and C, plus the plain tap water. The same was done with the four lettuce plants. Make sure you know which plant is getting which water.

2) Check the plants every day for four weeks and write down what you notice about each plant's growth and health. Chart your observations.

PROCEDURE C

1) Using a fresh sample of rinse water from Detergent A, use water-testing strips to indicate some of the water's chemical contents. In the actual project, "four-way" water strips were used to test for bromine, free chlorine, pH, and total alkalinity. Write down the results.

2) Let the water sample sit uncovered for one week.

3) Use the same type of water strips to test the water sample again.

4) In the meantime, repeat Steps 1, 2, and 3 for the other two rinse water types, as well as the plain tap water control sample. Write down all results.

5) Chart and compare the results to see if there are any differences between fresh rinse water and week-old rinse water.

<u>CONCLUSIONS</u>

Hypothesis 1 was wrong. A detergent with bleach seemed to help sprout the most seeds the soonest.

Hypothesis 2 was wrong. All plants grew and thrived. Bleach seemed to be no factor at all.

Hypothesis 3 was wrong. There were chemical differences in the rinse water after it sat for a week.

<u>WHAT IT MEANS IN THE REAL WORLD</u>

When the clouds refuse to spill, washing-machine rinse water may have some real recycling potential in growing garden plants. Further testing is necessary to learn if plants are safe to eat after being grown this way. After all, nobody likes a bean salad that tastes like a mouthful of soap.

How Heavy Is That Horse?

WHERE THE IDEA CAME FROM
Really Wanting to Know What Your Horse Weighs

How do you weigh a huge, four-legged animal like a horse? "C'mere horsey, horsey, climb up on these four scales, now. Good horsey." Uh, nope. That's not how it's done. Unless you have expensive special scales, you can't really weigh a horse. Many horse owners just measure the horse's girth (the distance around its chest at its widest point) to estimate the horse's weight. But what if your dad told you about a mathematical tool he uses at work that lets him estimate the price of buildings by multiplying their length, width, age, and many other variables? Could multiplying a horse's length, width, age, and other things help you figure out how much it weighs? Hmmm. Something to wonder about as you clippity-clop along during your riding lessons.

ACTUAL PROJECT TITLE

"A Better 'Weigh' for Horses"

QUESTION

Is there a better way to estimate the weight of a horse than by just measuring its girth?

HYPOTHESIS

Horses' weights can be estimated more accurately by using more variables like girth, length, height, age, breed, and gender in a mathematical formula.

PROCEDURE

The first step in a project like this is to seek help. Contact a veterinarian or a teacher in a college veterinary school and explain what you want to do. You would want to find out as much as possible about your dad's mathematical technique (just so you know, it's called multiple regression analysis). A few friendly phone calls to vets and college mathematics teachers can set the stage for an amazing project like the following:

1) Measure the girth, height, and length of 75 horses and take down all the details about each horse's age, breed, and gender. (Seventy-five horses! See why you need to call a vet?)

2) Estimate the weight of all these horses in the usual way, using the girth measurements.

3) Weigh each horse using regular horse scales to get an accurate weight. (See why you need to call a veterinary school?)

4) Because you now know each horse's actual weight, you know whether the girth measurement technique is accurate. What's more, because you know not only the actual weight, but the girth, height, age, breed, and gender, you can see how these details relate to the horse's actual weight. Time to put that handy multiple regression analysis tool to work. (And time to call that math professor, don't you think?)

5) With the help of the math professor and computer software, use your horse measurements and actual weights to come up with a mathematical formula. You want to be able to enter the horse measurements on one side of the formula and get the horse's weight on the other side.

6) Compare the accuracy of your formula to the accuracy of the other weighing methods.

CONCLUSION

The hypothesis is correct. Using more than just a single girth measurement can give you a much more accurate estimate of a horse's weight. Just in case you're wondering, the formula, worked out with the help of a math professor, turned out to be: **Girth x Girth x Length x .0000397397 + 244.200732 = Horse's Weight.** Not bad for a seventh grader, huh?

WHAT IT MEANS IN THE REAL WORLD

Being able to accurately weigh a horse without a scale is important to veterinarians or farmers watching weight gain or loss in horses. It can also be used by horse trainers at racetracks. But it's much more than that. The idea that hearing about a formula for estimating the price of buildings can lead to a formula for estimating the weight of horses is science at its best. Who knows where it can go from here? Ever wonder what elephants at the zoo really weigh?

About That Shrimp...

WHERE THE IDEA CAME FROM
Scary TV News Reports About Shrimp

Like many other good foods, shrimp can go bad. That's because while people love to eat shrimp, so do bacteria. When bacteria get there first, watch out. Humans who eat the bacteria will soon be making lots of noise in the bathroom. Supermarkets sell different types of cooked shrimp. Sometimes it is cooked and frozen in factories and stays frozen until you bring it home and thaw it out. Sometimes the store cooks the shrimp and sells it on ice, but not frozen. Is one type safer than the other? Figuring out where the bacteria is—and isn't—might mean less worry and more fun when "shrimp night" rolls around.

ACTUAL PROJECT TITLE
"Comparative Analysis of Bacterial Levels in Cooked Shrimp"

QUESTION
Which has more bacteria—store-cooked shrimp or factory-cooked shrimp?

HYPOTHESIS

Store-cooked and packaged shrimp, stored on ice, will have more bacteria than factory-cooked, frozen shrimp.

PROCEDURE

It took a lot of research and hard work, but this project followed as closely as possible the methods a professional microbiologist would use in testing foods for bacteria. The procedure included learning to use laboratory blenders, precise methods for incubation, a special device called a stomacher bag, peptone water, and everybody's favorite microbiology culture media—nonselective medium tryptic soy agar. Five brands of shrimp were tested to professional standards over an eight-day period.

USING YOUR ADVANTAGES

This project is special because the eighth-grade student learned and used all the techniques of a professional microbiologist. The student had an unusual advantage—her mother had been a nurse in Azerbaijan (find it on your world map!), where regular nurses often perform tests that, in most countries, would be handled by specialists. Is it okay to learn from a parent or other person with experience while you do a science fair project? Of course. It's called using your advantages.

CONCLUSION

Shrimp cooked in the store had high levels of food-spoiling bacteria, as well as bacterial contamination possibly caused by humans. Very serious types of bacteria were not found in any of the shrimp.

WHAT IT MEANS IN THE REAL WORLD

As noted earlier, besides all the science, one of the main reasons scientists go to huge international symposiums is for the giant platters of shrimp they serve at the receptions. This project shows it's probably better to eat the shrimp that was cooked and frozen at the factory than the shrimp that was cooked and put on ice at the store. Next time you're at one of those big shrimp parties, you might want to casually ask one of the waiters: "So... sure is some good-looking shrimp.... Did you get it frozen?"

More Inspiration

50 Actual Titles of Fifth- through Eighth-Grade Science Fair Projects That Won School, Regional, and National Awards

Now that you're an expert on using the scientific method, you can probably visualize a whole science fair project at a moment's notice. Think we're kidding? Here's a chance to prove your new abilities. Spend a few minutes with these various award-winning project titles dreamed up by kids just like you. Skip around as much as you like. Chances are you can now read some of these titles and immediately begin to imagine science fair projects that might go with them. Give it a try. If you can't do it yet, no problem. It just means you need to read the book again. Ha-ha!

1. Strength of Spider Silk
2. The Effects of Age on Learning Ability
3. Which Fresh-Flower Preservative Works Best?
4. Cats: Left- or Right-Pawed?
5. Lung Capacity, Jumper vs. Non-Jumper
6. Do Paper Airplanes of Various Paper Types Stay Aloft for Different Amounts of Time?
7. Which Additive Most Increases the Size of Soap Bubbles?
8. Listen Up: Testing the Effectiveness of Ear Plugs
9. Beetle Juice
10. Talkin' Trash from Garbage to Gas
11. Not Too Crabby: Predator-Prey Relationship in the Mystic River
12. Do You See What I See?
13. Slime and Other Fluids—What Makes Them Stick!
14. Dirty Money: An Investigation of Bacterial Growth on Currency
15. The Effects of Light Pollution and Beach Nourishment on Sea Turtles
16. Magnets and Lasers: No Smoke and Mirrors!
17. Snail Trails: Can Fruit Enzymes Be Used to Control Garden Snails?

Selected Bibliography

Amato, Carol, and Eric Ladizinsky. *50 Nifty Science Fair Projects*. Los Angeles: Lowell House, 1993.

Barron, John. *The Parent's Guide to Science Fairs*. Lincolnwood, IL: Lowell House, 1999.

Kramer, Stephen P. *How to Think like a Scientist: Answering Questions by the Scientific Method*. New York: Thomas Y. Crowell Junior Books, 1987.

Tocci, Salvatore. *How to Do a Science Fair Project*. Revised edition. New York: Franklin Watts, 1997.

Tucker, Tom. *Brainstorm! The Stories of Twenty American Kid Inventors*. New York: Farrar, Straus and Giroux, 1995.

VanCleave, Janice. *Janice VanCleave's Guide to the Best Science Fair Projects*. New York: John Wiley & Sons, 1997.

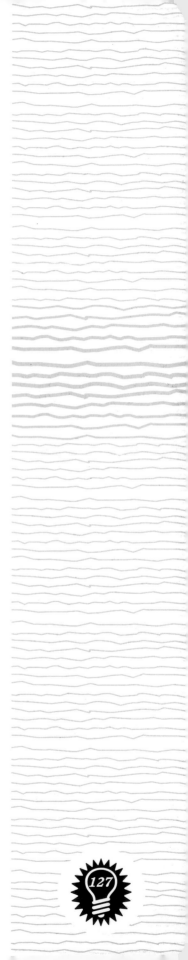

Metric System Conversion Tables

Linear Measure (Length)

If You Have	Multiply by	to Get
Inches	2.540	Centimeters
Feet	0.305	Meters
Yards	0.914	Meters
Miles	1.609	Kilometers

Square Measure (Area)

If You Have	Multiply by	to Get
Square inches	6.452	Square centimeters
Square feet	0.093	Square meters
Square yards	0.836	Square meters

Cubic Measure (Volume)

If You Have	Multiply by	to Get
Cubic inches	16.387	Cubic centimeters
Cubic feet	0.028	Cubic meters
Cubic yards	0.765	Cubic meters

Liquid Measure

If You Have	Multiply by	to Get
Fluid ounces	29.574	Milliliters
Fluid ounces	0.029	Liters
Quarts	0.946	Liters
Gallons	3.785	Liters

METRIC TO U.S. CONVERSION

Linear Measure (Length)

If You Have	Multiply by	to Get
Centimeters	0.393	Inches
Meters	3.281	Feet
Meters	1.094	Yards
Kilometers	0.621	Miles

Square Measure (Area)

If You Have	Multiply by	to Get
Square centimeters	0.155	Square inches
Square meters	10.764	Square feet
Square meters	1.196	Square yards

Cubic Measure (Volume)

If You Have	Multiply by	to Get
Cubic centimeters	0.061	Cubic inches
Cubic meters	35.315	Cubic feet
Cubic meters	1.308	Cubic yards

Liquid Measure

If You Have	Multiply by	to Get
Milliliters	0.034	Fluid ounces
Liters	33.824	Fluid ounces
Liters	1.057	Quarts
Liters	0.264	Gallons

Index